The freedom of years

The Bible Reading Fellowship
15 The Chambers, Vineyard
Abingdon OX14 3FE
brf.org.uk

The Bible Reading Fellowship (BRF) is a Registered Charity (233280)

ISBN 978 0 85746 506 1
First published 2018
10 9 8 7 6 5 4 3 2 1 0

Acknowledgements
Unless otherwise acknowledged, scripture quotations from the Good News Bible
published by The Bible Societies/HarperCollins Publishers Ltd, UK © American Bible
Society 1966, 1971, 1976, 1992, used with permission.

Extracts from the Authorised Version of the Bible (The King James Bible), the rights
in which are vested in the Crown, are reproduced by permission of the Crown's
Patentee, Cambridge University Press.

Every effort has been made to trace and contact copyright owners for material used
in this resource. We apologise for any inadvertent omissions or errors, and would
ask those concerned to contact us so that full acknowledgement can be made in
the future.

A catalogue record for this book is available from the British Library

Printed and bound by CPI Group (UK) Ltd, Croydon CR0 4YY

Harriet & Donald Mowat

The freedom of Years

Ageing in perspective

For our fathers,
Jim and Donald

Contents

Acknowledgements

Many people have helped us with this book: patients, health and social care colleagues, older people living in residential care, ageing family and friends, as well as countless others who have written about ageing in different contexts. We have learnt from them all. We are particularly grateful to Janice Whittick, who read a draft very carefully and gave us wise counsel, and to our editor, Mike Parsons, who helped us keep our anxieties under control.

Our fictional characters Angus and Josephine, whose life courses run throughout the book, are made by an amalgamation of many people we have met along the way. We have used many observed characteristics and experiences to develop their stories. They are no one in particular and everyone in some part.

All mistakes in this book are made by us, but we have tried to keep these to a minimum. We have used both feminine and masculine pronouns to make general statements. Occasionally, some of our older quotes use the generic 'man' and, in these cases, we have changed this to 'humanity'.

Harriet and Donald Mowat, 2018

Introduction

Discussion of the 'ageing population' seems to be everywhere these days. We can't watch the news without hearing about pressures on emergency services, bed blocking or the rising costs of care homes. Politicians seem to struggle to define or agree on the 'problem': no one is sure which group of professionals is to blame. All of them agree that time and resources are in short supply. What are we to make of this very contemporary crisis in our Western world?

Taking a spiritual perspective arguably gives us a focus, and helps us move to the core of what is important to people. Ours is specifically a Christian perspective developed within the UK's health and social care services over the past 40 years; although we hope still to hold the interest of the secular reader, our national services have evolved in the 20th century out of a Christian culture in Western Europe and, despite the pressures of political correctness in the new century, it seems difficult to ignore these determinants.

Perhaps you visit a spouse or relative in hospital or a care setting? Perhaps, like us, you have begun to think about the nature of your own ageing: that, just possibly, in time to come, those 'old people' will prove to be us? Perhaps you work as a care attendant or nurse? Perhaps you are a volunteer, attached to a church and visiting elders from your community in such a setting? You may be a hospital chaplain, a vicar, or a bewildered and stressed social worker or medic. You may well have reached your 50s and beyond, and have started to think about your own ageing journey.

Angus and Josephine, fictional characters whom you will meet during this book, are, we hope, illustrative of the way different formative experiences confer different perspectives on life, shape further life experience and potentially influence different health outcomes. There are many facets to ageing, and we take time in these pages to discuss the psychological and social aspects as they affect us as individuals in context, from early life attachments and through our attempts at personal maturation, to what is sometimes called 'successful ageing'. We talk about the contemporary social context that affects us and our lives in relation to family, to caring institutions and to professionals as we age, as gradually 'they' become 'us'.

What are we to make of things? We all search for meaning, through our own and one another's stories and narratives. As Angus and Josephine's stories unfold, perhaps alongside the stories of your own loved ones, we have an opportunity to think about ageing, its discontents and its effects on our own spirits and spirituality.

Why bother? Ageing is an issue long brushed under the rug, by politicians and by those of us (most of us) who prefer denial to facing reality. This book, we hope, will help you to develop the strength to deal with difficult feelings and difficult realities concerning the contemporary care of elders. Through knowing our ageing selves a little better, we will learn to look before we leap. We offer help here in understanding more fully the lives of our elders and the context in which those lives have been shaped and led, and in understanding better how to enhance what is already going well, without our getting in the way.

We hope that we have written a readable book, one which is robust when it comes to its basic ideas. We have tried, in the light of new knowledge in the field of neurobiology, to relate this to more generally accepted psychology and theology. This is a complicated area and deserves wider attention and debate in a society increasingly oriented towards work and materialism. The growing understanding that both psychological and spiritual phenomena arise from and are integrated in a biological context challenges the idea of distinctions between mind, body and spirit, which has dominated Western thinking for centuries.

Our book flows from the general to the specific, finishing with a summary chapter. The first chapter introduces Angus and Josephine, who accompany us throughout the book. We think initially about the way in which we understand ageing; in the second chapter, we look in more detail at what the purpose of ageing might be. Chapters 3 and 4 examine accepted ideas about successful ageing and the links between ageing and spiritual journeys. In Chapters 5 and 6, we build some social policy and political context around our ageing and current societal attitudes to this. Chapter 7 acts as a bridge into the second half of the book, focusing on some of the difficulties that we might experience as we age. Chapters 8 and 9 are grounded in what we come to call the 'second half' of life; we look there at the possibilities of doing things differently as we age, at how this can be encouraged and supported, and at the freedom that might result if, as chapter 10 concludes, we can put at least some accrued virtues into practice, and leave 'good stories' behind us.

Chapter 1

We are all ageing

Whenever I see someone, may I never feel superior. From the depth of my heart, may I be able to really appreciate the other person in front of me. Whenever I am with kings, presidents or beggars, I always remember we are the same.

You were born the same human way. There is no special way that bishops are born, and when the end comes, also you will die as a normal human being.[1]

The old-age dilemma

Just before Christmas 2015, our beloved Labrador Holly had to be put down. Those who have loved dogs know how difficult this can be. Holly was an old lady with severe osteoarthritis. She had had a wonderful, trouble-free life with us for her twelve years; she had come to no harm and nothing unpleasant had happened to her, save the odd denial of a dog biscuit and occasional shout of fury as she shook herself all over us after being in the sea. She provided us and all our children with enormous quantities of love, amusement and joy over her life. We have always had two dogs at a time, and now we find ourselves with only one, with our equally beloved 'rescue' Labrador, Rupert. His life has not been as serene or assured; perhaps after traumas in earlier life, he came to us aged four, angry and distressed, and took a while to trust us.

We are all missing Holly, especially Rupert, and we show it in different ways. Rupert is quieter, we are a shade sadder and there seems to be something missing: something just around the corner that we can't quite grasp – something not quite right. Of course, these feelings will pass, but the associated set of discussions and feelings prompted by Holly's death are highly relevant to this book.

Should we find another puppy? A new Labrador will probably live a similar time, between 12 and 14 years, and by that time we will be in our late 70s. What will our lives look like by then? Would it be 'responsible' of us to embark on adopting another dog 'at our stage of life'? When is someone too old to have a dog? We're quite sure we *will* get another dog, such is the emotional power of hope and joy over 'responsible and sensible' rationality. But the discussion we are having raises deeper questions about our ageing selves, and the degree to which we are all influenced in our decision-making by the stereotypes and assumptions associated with old age. It also makes us conscious of uncomfortable realities about the passage of time, and requires us to face up to our own ageing.

Questions of meaning

It seems that we all inevitably come, at some stage in our life, to the question of our meaning and place in the world. We begin to ask ourselves, 'What is life all about? What is it all *for*?' More pressingly, 'What has *my* life been about, and what does the future hold, both in this world and in any future life after death?' In most cases, this will be a revisit, probably, of the questions wrestled with in our youth in one way or another, as we propelled ourselves (or were propelled, if we lacked drive) into the wider world.

These questions, 'What is my life about, and what am I going to do about it?', are the key to managing and giving substance to one's life. We each have our different versions and timings of these existential questions, and of course we each respond differently to life's prompts. For most of us, these issues become sidelined by our movement into that middle period of life, where we seem to be swallowed up by worldly concerns. Our 'generative years', as the Eriksons called them,[2] require us to look out to the world, to produce, to thrust ourselves forwards. In these middle years, we are ensnared in productivity of one kind or another. We get our meaning, if we have time to think about it, from our culturally agreed 'generative purposes', including educating ourselves, making money to live and thrive, buying houses, building lives with each other. We cultivate interests, we might produce children and care for them. We might care for our elders. But do we do all this thoughtfully, or simply according to economic vogue, to the politics and culture of the day?

Questions of meaning, mortality and death inevitably pop up throughout our lives, often from the unconscious in the form of dreams, shy reminders of what might be important. These questions often come unexpectedly, out of the blue, sometimes as a natural consequence of a response to life events. Perhaps a contemporary of ours dies, surprisingly and suddenly, and this causes us to think about our own death. It brings us up short, catches us unawares and reminds us of the reality of our own fragility. Our parents age: we watch them growing frailer, perhaps becoming more cautious and probably experiencing a variety of aches and pains or long-term disability, a portent perhaps for our own lives. Our parents die, and this causes us to consider our own ageing selves and our inevitable mortality. All around us there is a background media drone about the ageing population, about the difficulties and problems associated with ageing: we reluctantly, after much resistance, begin to think about our own personal ageing. We wonder *when* we should consider ourselves old. 'Is it about age or attitude?' we muse. The 'forever young' approach of the advertising world and the insistences of the 'baby boomer' generation seem hollow, and collapse soundlessly in the face of practical realities, after the echoing assertions that we are 'worth it' die away.

It is part of our shared human condition and experience to ask these questions. How we respond and deal with such questions is the general subject of this book. The way in which our ageing helps or hinders us in thinking about these questions of meaning is its specific context. We take the view that ageing is part of life, and requires us therefore to think about life and its meaning, a view shared with Helen Small, who writes simply: 'If we want to think differently about old age, then we have to think differently about life itself.'[3]

Our Christian perspective

We have written this book from our shared Christian perspective, which combines backgrounds in Church of Scotland and Anglican traditions. We hope that won't discourage people of other faiths, or those of no professed religious affiliation. In any case, our perspective won't be every Christian's idea of Christianity, and 'ours' does not claim any great authority, other than as an expression or outcome of our thinking, praying and searching over many years. We want this book simply to be one contribution, and a stimulant to thought about ageing.

Our initial idea for a title to hold together our ideas on ageing was 'living without triumph'. This concept has become central to our own thinking about living and ageing. The phrase is taken from a passage written by our friend David Ogston.[4] David was a man of great sensitivity, joy, insight and agony; after his death, his wife, Meg, and his friend and clerical colleague Johnston McKay sifted through the treasury of his writings, creating two volumes of prayer, poetry and thought. David had been pondering upon what he called 'the refractions of Jesus': borrowing from John le Carré, he imaginatively categorises these as 'Tinker, Tailor, Soldier and Spy', writing about the changing ideas and realities of Christians as soldiers. The old references to 'onward', 'marching as to war', 'putting on the armour' and 'fighting a good fight with all [their] might', he feels, are increasingly less relevant and less understandable. Things are just not like that any longer:

This is not where the Christian is, not at all… Most of the time the Christian feels as if he or she is actually a member of some forgotten army… Christians are a timid and shuffling group who argue amongst themselves and get sidetracked with trivia, whilst all the while feeling they are on a great campaign.

He points out the tension and paradox between the Christians' love of triumph, and the knowledge and bitter experience of defeat. He refers to St Ignatius of Loyola's prayer:

Dearest Lord, teach me to be generous;
Teach me to serve Thee as Thou deservest;
To give and not to count the cost;
To fight and not to heed the wounds;
To toil and not to seek for rest;
To labour and not to seek reward,
Save that of knowing that I do Thy will.

This prayer, David Ogston suggests, describes what it feels like to be a lonely army of one. However, it is in the occupation of this loneliness, of this place of uncertainty, in thinking about where the battle *is* that the individual might deserve congratulation, might merit any sense of experiencing triumph. It is in the loneliness and the steadfastness despite uncertainty, in the battle within ourselves for meaningful peace or lasting sense of achievement, that the learning takes place. We learn eventually to live without triumph, without inflation, without hubris, without grandiosity. Instead, we are left with a sense that the collective good matters far more than our individual accomplishment. Those who can achieve *this* balance are those who are at last truly putting on the armour of God.

We have taken this analytic view and extended it to include the journey into ageing. David talks about the tensions within our hymns, our worship and our thoughts. When we are finally learning to live without necessary reference to worldly achievement and to its material trappings, we are 'living without triumph'. When we can recognise and learn to resist the temptations of power, envy, vanity and gluttony, we are beginning to live by different criteria. Later we will refer to Richard Rohr's thinking about being *in the flow*,[5] which also pursues the idea of living in relationship, rather than in hierarchical opposition to each other. We may dare to speak of 'putting on the armour of Christ' to enter old age, as we enter a dance with each other and with God. This will give us a chance to revisit and review our core beliefs. We will need help with this.

Christians who don't go to church

Our approach in this book has also been influenced by the recent discussions of and interest in the 'invisible' church.[6] This is a term used by Steve Aisthorpe to describe people who are Christians but who do not attend church any more. Aisthorpe suggests that a significant group of people have a strong Christian faith, but either have stopped going to church or have rarely attended formal church. Most of this group are in their 50s and beyond. His book is a wake-up call to churches who focus on attendance as the mark of faithfulness, and who fix on youth policy as the one means of keeping church going. Linda Woodhead has written extensively on the phenomenon of declining religious adherence, and the rise in its place of alternative spiritual interest and 'no religion'.[7]

Aisthorpe and Woodhead's ideas of faith involving doubt and disbelief are not new, of course, but they alert us once again to the profound, compelling, lifelong and ever-changing nature of the Christian journey of faith, a journey ultimately inseparable from that of ageing. People do, it is readily observed, move away from institutionalised religious activity towards a more mixed economy of Christian and spiritual practices, and we might do well to see this as part of the Christian journey, rather than (through an arguably authoritarian lens) simply as a failure to adhere. We discuss in our conclusions the specific implications of this dilemma for the way the church might choose to act in relation to spiritual care for older people who are disabled or incapacitated in some way. So, while we acknowledge the importance and centrality of church life and services to many, we attempt to think about Christian care more broadly, beyond the confines of church behaviours and practices.

Some difficult questions

Part of our search as ageing Christians is to find ways of ageing well and 'successfully'. In Chapter 3, we think in a bit more detail about the ideas on successful ageing and the links to the 'anti-ageing' voice so prevalent in our society. This voice invokes memories of the myth of Narcissus, his self-absorption, his rejection of all external influences other than his compliant and cowardly companion, Echo, and his dependence on his mirrored reflection, which leads inexorably to his downfall. Myths exist to help us think. There is an understandable wish, as we age, to look for a recipe or a simple formulation, a way of ageing that will be successful for us without disturbing our comfort or our complacency: indeed, a whole field of social and medical research exists calling itself 'successful ageing', although thankfully the irony of this is not lost, and it is suitably critical of itself.

'Successful' is a rather problematic concept, in any case: one person's success may obviously be another person's failure. Is it, for instance, a mark of success to live a long life, making it to one's late 90s? This must surely depend on quality of life. How do we measure this? Whose success are we marking? Is it that of genetics, social environment, family or even God? If a woman is confined to bed, unresponsive through advanced dementia, flexing in pain, finding daylight a trial, then one might argue that this is not a particularly successful ageing trajectory even if, as a centenarian, she can briefly or meaningfully glance across at a telegram. When do we stop counting birthdays? These ideas imply difficult discussions to be had, often resulting in decisions being deferred to clinical staff. One woman's idea of quality of life may be the dread of another. Dare we ask: is it the destination or the journey that is important?

We are all heading to one destination: 'Dust you are and to dust you will return' (Genesis 3:19, NIV). This dust is our universal experience; we will all die, and we all age, no matter our age at death. How we journey to our death through life is, however, entirely unique, and we really are offered endless hope, possibilities of love and grounds for strengthening faith. Although there are many shared stages and paths along the way, the road that each of us ultimately takes is an individual one. And what we learn on the way is the vital thing.

Two approaches to ageing

In our research and clinical experience over the years, we have informally identified two very broad 'types' of agers: firstly, people who think about ageing, who make changes and who embark on an inner life, and, secondly, people who retain their midlife *modus vivendi*, thereby choosing to sustain what we might call the outward journey. Let's look at two differing examples.

Introducing ANGUS...

Angus is in his early 80s. He was recently widowed after 50 years of a happy marriage to his late wife, Sally. He has two children and four grandchildren, all of whom know, love and regularly maintain contact with him. He is financially secure and can afford holidays and treats. He spends a lot of time with friends, in the village in which he has lived for much of his adult life. He is a welcome invitee to parties and events. He is charming and amusing, as well as very accepting of others; he tells a good joke. He is well educated, good-looking and genuinely modest about his accomplishments and the considerable contribution he has made to village life. He enjoys social company and is very gregarious.

He has been a churchwarden, and he is still involved in the social life of the church. He goes to church every week but admits, when pushed, to having little substantial 'belief'. His image of God is rather childlike: he pictures God as an old man on a cloud, a benign being but without much connection with his people on earth (God, not Angus, he laughs without any sense of irony). He has no idea where his wife is in her death. He hopes she is warm and comfortable.

Life has not demanded much reflection from Angus. Indeed, he says he is not psychologically minded. He finds that, although he can be cheerful and upbeat when he is in company, when home alone in the evening he cannot go upstairs to bed because of an overwhelming sense of loss. Nights are dark and lonely, and he is full of fear. He displays this by refusing to eat alone, for fear that he chokes when there is no one close by to help him. This fear reflects ancient memories of a fellow university student, who had made it through a difficult World War II only to die by choking on a biscuit as he sat alone in his digs. Angus' memory of this, and the accompanying anxiety, is reflected in a difficulty in swallowing generally. He is consulting the family doctor about this. Outwardly, he is 'great for his age'; inwardly, his spiritual journey is faltering and uncomfortable. He is discontented, he is frightened and he is profoundly lonely.

Introducing JOSEPHINE...

By contrast, let us think about Josephine, who is 96 years of age. She is a lay nun, belonging to an order that is scattered across the country. Her lay community is growing older and fewer in number, and they mostly communicate by letter or phone. Josephine has a degree from Cardiff, conferred between the two World Wars. She was a missionary in Africa for many years, living in difficult and challenging conditions. She never married or had children. Upon retirement, she lived in a van on the outskirts of a village before moving into her present rented accommodation as she became less mobile and consequently unable to drive.

She acted as verger to the local church for years, responsible for locking and unlocking the church. She fell on the steps of the church because of increased frailty and broke her leg, which caused her final retreat into being housebound. Her living accommodation is an unmodernised two-room flat which contains an old sink, a scullery and a bedroom/sitting room. This has ill-fitting French windows that open on to an unkempt garden. Josephine loves the garden and encourages the wildlife into the house; mice, cats and birds are all welcome. She is incontinent of urine at night, and has cataracts that she will not have removed because she fears (understandably) that admission into hospital will precipitate an insistence that she move into residential care. The authorities, she says, are desperate to get her out of her home, whereas she wishes fervently to remain. She washes her own bedclothes by hand and dries them in front of her gas fire. She is accustomed to (and therefore unaware of) the smell of infected urine, which is overpowering to visitors. She knows that the district nurse team are worried about her safety, and are keen to move her on. She feels under siege.

She has good neighbours, who bring her soup and meals. Her daily living is a precarious balancing act. She has a home help, who does what she can. Josephine has a daily prayer schedule, which she performs as part of her religious community duties. This means that she insists that visitors and official 'help' must make an appointment to see her. Her relationship with God is tangible and very present. She is in control of her*self*.

Angus and Josephine are having different experiences of ageing, but also share the common threads that bind us together as we grow older. They are both experiencing loss of freedom, in one form or another. The response to this loss of freedom is very different in each 'case', as it is to some extent in the 'cases' of each individual we encounter.

We will revisit Angus and Josephine many times during this book and their stories will unfold as we do so.

Disassociation from ageing: managing our fears

Of course, our patterns of ageing reflect our patterns of living: the two are inextricably linked. The kind of personhood each of us exhibits in youth and in old age tends to remain constant, sometimes even when we have striven to make changes; personality, insofar as it can be measured (a practical possibility nowadays, many authorities assert), does not change very much over a lifetime.

Developmental psychology is helpful in providing a framework for us to think about our own ageing. Melanie Klein describes two extreme psychological positions adopted by people of any age, two psychological lenses that we use to occupy, understand and importantly to manage our world.[8] First, she describes the 'paranoid-schizoid' position; essentially, this stance is a defensive position, where understanding of the world and ourselves within it requires judgement of others as good or bad, right or wrong. This is, of course, a very concrete way of our looking at the world, a view of the world that privileges certainty and absolutes. In this world, should she so choose it, an individual would tend to locate herself by way of comparison with others; for example, in this mindset, for me to think of myself as beautiful, slim and gifted, you would need to be less beautiful, less slim or less gifted than me; for me to be clever, you would need to be seen as being less clever, and so on. For me to be right, you must be wrong; for me to have the toy, you can't have it. For me to be ageing well, you must be ageing less well. Even though we are the same age, I look so much younger than you do, and am therefore probably a better person than you. (An alternative mindset, we shall see, might of course acknowledge that we are both ageing individuals, doing the best we can.)

One of our grandmothers gave a classic illustration of this, while she was an elderly woman living in a care home. She insisted on our helping 'that old woman over there' who was struggling with her coat. While this made us laugh, what was really going on was that Grandma saw herself as different, specifically not the same as the other older woman, whereas we from our younger perspective saw these two older women as very similar. Identifying this difference between her and the other older woman was important to Grandma, and helped her feel good about herself. This goodness was dependent on not being as old or infirm as the others. Age itself became a bad thing, almost a moral failing. This way of seeing the world is very common.

Klein's theory of human development suggests that developmental maturation, rather like ballet, involves a shift to a second, less extreme position, where one can be more accepting of both similarity and difference. This second position Klein calls the 'depressive position': a more 'mature' position, which we can easily see seems more restful and less exhausting for all concerned. I can be beautiful and you can be beautiful too, but in different ways. I can share my toys with you without feeling compromised. I can be right or wrong about things, irrespective of what others think or feel. And there can be negotiation: I can, perhaps like you, be both a little bit right and a little bit wrong. My 'goodness' need no longer be determined by others' 'badness'. I can experience my ageing in various ways over time, without having to set myself up in competition with other ageing people. My world might perhaps be a little less exciting with this perspective, less combative and competitive; it also becomes a world of uncertainty and compromise, but it arguably offers a much more manageable, more peaceful and less exhausting psychological situation. Klein, of course, portrayed this as a dynamic, rather than a once-and-for-all shift, with individuals moving positions according to circumstances and stresses.

We can see how this dynamic is specifically applicable to ageing. For me to feel younger and good about my (possibly immature) self and my unusually unwrinkled face, you must look older and have more wrinkles. Pressed by our Western culture, we all tend to think other people are ageing, while somehow we are not. For we, it seems, are 'worth it'. We spot people on television who seem to us to have aged (often once-famous actresses in ads for make-up), and we gladly persuade ourselves that we have not aged in the same way. It is only when we catch our former bloom in an old photograph or see our current image in the mirror, and find our mother or father looking back at us, that the reality of ageing momentarily looms up into consciousness, before being hurriedly repressed. Our sense of personal immortality is hard to lose.

It seems, then, that we need a sense of endlessness, of eternity, to plan and live in some sort of balance with our culture. We also need a sense of mortality, for just the same reason! Finding this balance is one of the tasks of ageing (see Chapter 8). Speaking to one of our daughters about what our situation might be in 20 years' time, and realising that one or both of us might well be dead by then, having lived full and healthy lives to 85, came as quite a shock to us. We seem to need to hang on to our immortality and to our sense of a unique position in the world. The fact that we are all ageing, that we are all the same, is a difficult lesson to learn. Of course, the truth is that although we are all the same, we are also unique – all entirely different in our experience of that same inevitable route.

In the next chapter, we will think in more detail about the nature of ageing, how the psychological arises from the biological and how it determines to some extent our experience of ageing. Eventually, inevitably, often reluctantly, we come to the question of our meaning and place in the world. What is life all about? What has my life been about, and what does the future hold, both in this world and after my death? It is best that we do at least some of this questioning before rushing to impose our half-baked ideas on others. For us to be well and to age well, things must change as we grow older. Our outlook on and approach to the world should alter. Should you doubt this, just imagine if we were condemned to remain as adolescents! We are required to become resilient: resilience means being realistic, finding a meaning to our lives and being creative with our lives.

Carl Jung, psychiatrist and psychotherapist, said:

> We cannot live the afternoon of life according to the programme of life's morning: for what was great in the morning will be little at evening, and what in the morning was true, will at evening have become a lie.[9]

Walking the ageing path together, old and young, carer and cared-for can tell their stories. Conversations help us to reinterpret the past, to understand more truly what happened to us in the light of another's opinion. Therefore, we talk to each other, and not just to therapists. We 'improve our biographies', to paraphrase James Hillman, an American psychologist who we will come to later. We can begin to understand the past and the future better and, more importantly, to live more fully in the present. Carers or cared-for, we must share the restless journey of our lives.

Chapter 2

What is ageing for?

The greatest moral question facing us in the 21st century is: what is ageing for?[10]

Is old age really included in the purposes of God?...

Nothing in nature encourages its old to exist longer than they can function for the good of their community. Indeed, I can find no living thing – other than humankind – that puts energy and resources into keeping old members alive once they have ceased to be 'of use' to others. Old elephants simply fall behind as the community moves on and the family leaves them to die of want. Old trees just wither, and become compost for their surrounding growth. Nothing else in nature puts up with ageing members relying on energy and time from younger generations who themselves are vital to their community as producers. Nor does anything created demand endless and exhausting 'care' from relatives who themselves are growing older.[11]

Thanks to a combination of social and economic advance, greater wealth, better nutrition and excellent technical healthcare, we now live longer than before. These changes leave us with new questions. How do we value our lives, and how can we best take on the new challenges of ageing? What are we to do with our 'freedom of years'? What is the best mindset to have in order to discipline ourselves to think about and meet this huge challenge? Our forebears were less well equipped, but now there are so many possible perspectives: theological, philosophical, biological and neuroscientific, with each discipline having something unique to offer. We have tried in our consideration to take something from each to light the way. If, like John Bunyan in *Pilgrim's Progress*, we keep to the tried-and-tested idea of life lived as *journey*, and view older age as an upcoming visit to a province new to us, then we are encouraged to think about how we can best be prepared for that place.

Although ageing is experienced differently by each of us and even then can be unpredictable, by a surprising number it is seen simply as a physical manifestation, a biological rundown, and this simple stance contains a fundamental, unavoidable truth. We all wrinkle, after all: our various capacities alter, whether physical, cognitive, intellectual or even emotional, and our dreams and aspirations change. But ageing is also a social construction, bringing undoubted privileges and accompanied by political connotations, such as pensions, leisure time, travel concessions and so on. You might find it helpful here to jot down a few of your own ideas of what ageing means to you; it can be valuable to have in mind and even to write down your own assumptions, which can often be generated in part by ungrounded fears.

Our preparation for ageing, as it happens, begins surprisingly early, in infancy, as we learn about love, security and ways of exploring the world. Recent advances in neuroscience related to aspects of parental nurture such as skin contact, cuddling, feeding and simple maternal presence have confirmed many of the ideas of an earlier generation of psychologists, in respect of their value for development, adult psychological well-being and a long and healthy life. In this chapter, we try to take the reader back over some of these quite complex concepts, simplifying where we can, and illustrating these ideas as they operate in the lives of Angus and Josephine. It may sound obvious, but for us to understand the situation of any older person we might try to help, we need firstly some understanding of what we now know about ageing; secondly, some insight into our own unique experience; and, thirdly, to know that person's own story and its influence on their thinking and actions. Listening to stories, we noted earlier, is a basic part of being human and is part of good practice in spiritual care, but what is essential is locating those stories in the context of love, and the loving experiences of the person. Love in the lives of others isn't always found in the places we would necessarily first assume. The past is always with us: our ageing journey incorporates it, and what goes on in our youth decidedly affects our ageing.

ANGUS and JOSEPHINE start out

Angus was born in Canada in 1920, to a young couple living in Manitoba. His father, Bill, a Canadian citizen, had met his mother, Esmé, in London late on in World War I. Bill was tall, good-looking in uniform, seemed to have plenty of money and was an excellent dancer. Esmé was less comfortable with herself, something of an outsider, and exhibited an awkwardness among her debutante friends; she fell heavily for Bill, who seemed to offer escape from her class-based restriction of options in a stuffy and authoritarian family atmosphere. There followed what used to be called a 'whirlwind romance', and after marrying they returned to run the family smallholding in Winnipeg, in 1919. Esmé gave birth to the beloved Angus without difficulty a year or two later, but had little practical family or social support; Bill's family were farmers, Christian Scientists from the prairie who didn't take easily to the need for nurture of a small baby and his upper-crust English mother, and were in any case preoccupied with the smallholding and the pressing need to eke a living from the cold ground. Things had been much easier for the family when Bill was in the military, earning and sending home money; now there were three other mouths to feed.

Esmé was from an upper-middle-class Anglican family who meanwhile took a dim view of the prospect of grandchildren growing up overseas, and her mother insisted on their return to England in 1923, when Angus was only two. Bill found a job with his father-in-law in the insurance business in the City of London, and amid much relief Esmé and little Angus were reabsorbed into the family. Thanks to Esmé's family's inherited wealth, schooling for Angus at Eton and Oxford followed. Angus served in the Canadian Army from 1942 to 1945, eventually graduating in history and (thanks to those family networks again) passing into a financial apprenticeship in fund management in the City in 1948.

Josephine's start in life, we might imagine, was somewhat different. She was born in 1918 to a Welsh Methodist couple living in Cardiff, not in poverty, but not in affluent circumstances either. Her father, John, had suffered from polio as a child and was exempted from conscription. He ran the family's butchery business in the absence of his father and uncle, who were 'in France' with the British Expeditionary Force, and had married her mother, Maureen, in 1917, not long after hearing of his own father's death in action at Verdun. The additional pressures of young Josephine and Maureen's needs, together with the emotional demands of his bereaved mother, were considerable and, by 1920, his heavy drinking had put the family business under great pressure, as did the births and subsequent demands of Josephine's three younger sisters.

Uncle Jim, returning as *paterfamilias* on surviving the war, took a dim view of John's situation but somehow managed to keep him occupied and the butchery business afloat. Uncle Jim encouraged John to volunteer in the Welsh Territorials despite his disabilities, where his natural orienteering skills were valued and would later make him useful to his country, despite his being 45 at the further outbreak of war with Germany. Josephine herself, the eldest of four, attended municipal schooling but was inevitably preoccupied by the needs of three younger sisters, her mother, Maureen, having died in childbirth in 1928. Josephine was forced, at ten, to grow up quickly. The pressures of coping with the girls inevitably limited her horizons, but she was bright and studious, could pass examinations and went on to do an MA at Cardiff, unusually for those times. She later served with the Salvation Army during the war, and took holy orders with the Franciscans in 1946. She was a missionary in Africa for much of her young adult life.

These two very different people of their time, Angus and Josephine, will, like all of us, go on in late older adulthood to present very different pictures, different characters, different personalities. Angus will turn out (in his 80s) to be active, independent, gregarious and sociable, the kind of man who is a welcome dinner guest, who doesn't trouble social services and who has ostensibly simple transactions with doctors. Josephine's situation will prove quite different, as future chapters will show: whatever her own internal psychological state, however 'spiritual' she feels, she will inevitably evoke anxieties in others, particularly publicly accountable professionals, as she will go on to become incontinent, to fall and to exhibit risk of fire in her 'independent' living.

Love is all you need

In his poem 'Little Gidding', T.S. Eliot reminds us that beginning and ending can be the other way around, and that we actually start from the end.[12] So our beginnings repay more detailed study; we should look first to the very earliest stages of ageing, prenatal life. We now know beyond doubt that experiences *in utero* affect the *ex utero* life chances of the baby. There is a complex biological interplay in pregnancy between mother and baby, at a time when a baby cannot make much in the way of distinctions among sensory experiences, when mind and body clearly cannot be separated, with babies vulnerable *in utero* to the wider maternal environment, such as maternal alcohol intake, the bone-chilling cold of the Canadian mid-western winter or the rages of an overburdened, angry father, as (we now know) stress hormones flood the placenta. Environmental factors alter the growth of the baby: the biological realities sit somewhat uneasily with the tranquil understanding offered to us by neo-classical images of a serene Madonna and Child. As a species, in comparison with animals, we humans are born helpless and need years of loving nurture and gradual fostering of independence to grow and develop to full health. The stakes are high for the mother-and-child twosome: love, in the form of warmth, feeding and holding (symbolised for us in the Madonna and Child) are vital to brain, and therefore emotional, development. So, choose your parents carefully: without these factors, a brain may fail to reach full size: low brain volume, modern neuroscience shows us, is linked to behavioural disturbance and antisocial behaviour in adult life.

More about attachment

Long before animal experimentation paved the way for hard science to make detailed measurement of human stress hormones, the psychological insights of first John Bowlby[13] and later Donald Winnicott[14] indicated the likely vital role of supportive maternal love and close contact with infants in early childhood in the underpinning of later human mental health and well-being. Although grudgingly held to be acceptable in the psychoanalytic fields of the 1960s and 1970s, their views were largely ignored in the wider spheres of medicine and society. These pioneers held that a child could increasingly explore, adventure and develop emotionally within a mother's orbit, in the reassuring certainty that mother is present, supporting and confirming the experiences, engaging in what is sometimes called 'reverie' (or early storytelling, amid much billing and cooing).

Further in the 'attachment' story we learn, initially through mammalian experimental work by Bowlby's associates, later confirmed by (ethically approved) analogous human experiments, that where there is sustained maternal inattention or absence, infants will exhibit *measurable abnormalities in feeding and social behaviour*, together with enhanced stress hormonal responses which are *prolonged into adulthood*. The implications for our resilience (or capacity for the virtue of fortitude) in later life are obvious: 'good enough' mothering, whether by the mother or indeed by some substitute figure, is vital even, we might say, if the 'mothering' turns out to be decades later in the life concerned, and even if the 'substitute mother' proves to be a psychotherapist, a daughter or a social carer. So, without a mother's gentle support of the child, allowing mutual loving gaze and reverie on the child's part amid early explorations of an environment, there can develop a degree of psychological trauma, manifesting later in life as adjustment difficulties, possible frank mental disorder or an evident need for relational repair.

This sheds light for us on why it might be vital to have some real understanding of one's own individual life story, its detail and, in time, the life stories of those we care for. More detail on all this is elegantly provided by Sue Gerhardt in *Why Love Matters*.[15] Gerhardt gives a compelling and sensitive account of the sweep of recent neuroscientific advances in human attachment theory, maternal loving and its dysfunction and implications. Extending these ideas, we unashamedly contend that love is the key to successful ageing. Loving, and feeling loved, is a hardwired prerequisite for managing one's life, for what the science increasingly calls 'self-regulation'. If we are privileged to be loved, we are more likely to be able to love, to awaken, to accept and enjoy the complexities of life.

Early life: learning to manage uncertainty

So, we've made it into the world and now we must engage in the world. We must find a way of understanding our world that faces the facts but doesn't overwhelm us. We will see later that, precisely to the extent to which our childhood experiences include love and nurturing, we will be able to manage complexity, suffering, joy and fleeting triumphs. We are thus either set fair (or not, alas) for our ageing journey. As we'll see in Chapter 8, the first half of this journey is outward, where things seem clear and certain (sometimes even despite quite severe early-life trauma). The 'second half' of life, the ageing journey on which this book is focused, is more complex; the way of life is often less clear, and certainty gives way to doubt. This latter part of the journey is, however, a gift to us, a blessing that allows us to grow closer to God the creator and, if we allow it, to understand better the relationship between suffering and faith. To fail to embark on that phase of life's journey is to remain in an earlier place, but inevitably without the comforts and hopes of youth. That can prove to be a desolate experience.

Let's return to think just a little more about those psychotherapists we mentioned, and what they might bring to the ideas of *nurture and ageing as personal development*. Many of their big ideas about how we think as people do seem to have everyday value, and consequently to have been absorbed into everyday awareness this past half-century. What seemed once to be sweeping and outlandish concepts now perhaps make more sense. Take for instance the thinking of Melanie Klein, whose work we introduced in Chapter 1. Klein taught that we develop unconscious fragments, ideas of 'good breast' and 'bad breast' in relation to our mother during attachment; if things went well for the baby, if she was well fed and held, then emotional contentment was registered, and represented in the emotional mind. If the breast was withheld, if there was controlled feeding for adult convenience, for example, then the internal emotional registration would be very different, coded unconsciously as Klein would have it as 'bad-breast' ideas. We shouldn't equate the primitive thinking of infants with that of adults, and we all remain somewhat hazy about what is conscious and what is unconscious, but Klein and many after her believed that, despite the undoubted courage of adults entering psychotherapeutic treatment, traces of primitive thinking, residues of infancy, can still be found in those adult clients, in their reported everyday interactions with people.

We saw in Chapter 1 Klein's suggestion that our thinking matured in time, from a binary, non-negotiable 'I am right, you are wrong' approach to something more like 'We are both probably a bit right and a bit wrong'. Klein saw as one aspect of maturation the developing ability to *hold the competing ideas of right and wrong, black and white in one more complex idea*. So those people who can accept grey as being 'a mixture of black and white' are likely to manage the complexities of the ageing journey better than those who rigidly stick to 'either black or white'. Carers of older people who can accept the muddle, risk and dignity of choice, together with the teetering uncertainties of a person's 'coping', will manage better and arguably will be better supports for older people than those more rigid individuals who must have things neat and tidy, certain and secure, and who interestingly often need someone to blame when things go awry. We will look more deeply at the idea of movement into the second half of life in Chapter 8: this process is essentially about learning to tolerate uncertainty, and about the acceptance of change.

Human developmental stages and the development of virtue

Erik Erikson, a painting tutor working in 1920s Vienna, met Freud's daughter Anna through his work teaching children, and was eventually persuaded to train in analysis. After moving to the US in 1932, Erikson went on to teach and practise at Harvard and Yale, publishing numerous books and papers on the staging or mapping of human psychological development, many with his wife, Joan. Their work is widely known and quoted in the field of developmental psychology: some of the ideas have had such extensive penetration into everyday thinking that they now pass unreferenced and are held to be 'common sense'. The Eriksons' early writings describe life in terms of maturational stages, and they tell of the challenges presented by life at each of these stages, particularly later life. Later in their own lives, the Eriksons worked with others to look at examples of these challenges in the lives of research subjects, incidentally but effectively demonstrating once again the central relevance of story.

The Eriksons' challenges are presented as *twin polarities*. Their idea is that each of these 'poles' (or extremes) needs to be experienced *and* felt by the individual, before *mastery over challenge* is achieved. It is in these experiences and clashes that a *virtue* (strength, or positive character attribute) emerges as new personal growth. For example, the young Angus, embarking on his working life as an apprentice in the financial world at 27, struggles away, learning to put into financial practice (as he learns to trade stocks) something of what he has learnt about the world through his history degree. This is the most natural thing in the world for this particular man in his 20s, purposefully learning to provide for a young wife and potentially a family, in a context where he knows inherently that he should try to justify the privileges he has been accorded through family money, status and a good education.

These features of Angus' story place him between Erikson's one challenge 'pole' of *initiative* and, on the other hand, Erikson's alternate pole of *guilt*. Angus is forced to wrestle with what he learned at Oxford beyond history, with what he has imbibed in the way of family story and myth, with the fact that life isn't easy, that Esme's family were more materially fortunate and privileged than Bill's, that life doesn't present itself as offering equality, and that there were many at Oxford who were intensely envious of him as a much-privileged young man, with an easy manner, a seemingly positive temperament, an effortless way with people and apparently a stellar trajectory into the most promising of careers. Not all of this was evident to him earlier. Angus feels this guilt of privilege with quite some intensity, and he must wrestle with these two elements of challenge until they are reconciled in him. When they *are* successfully reconciled, then he will have *grown* and will be stronger personally: he will prove to be a man of *purpose*, Erikson's recognisable virtue gained at this stage, because of this piece of wrestling undertaken.

We may incidentally be reminded of an Old Testament Jacob. Erikson clarifies for us that his described virtues are not presented as a 'tick list' of *achievements* to be had, but rather as the acquisition of natural personal characteristics, realised as the result of meeting and facing life's real challenges with authenticity. Erikson, a child analyst, initially placed his 'challenges' and virtue acquisitions mostly in childhood and early adult life, but he and his wife, Joan, revised and republished their expanded ideas over time as they themselves aged, acknowledging perhaps that there seemed to be much more going on in later life in the way of maturation than had been previously stated. Which of us couldn't agree with that?

So, beyond that one example in the life of Angus, what are these many 'challenges' outlined in the Eriksons' much-quoted and lively work, dynamically revisited and revised by the authors in their long lifetimes? We talked before about early-life experience, of Klein's good and bad breast. The Eriksons' earlier work anticipates one of Klein's 'big ideas' in their description of infant conflict concerning 'trust versus mistrust', producing an emergent virtue of *hope*. They also describe the second challenge of 'autonomy versus shame and doubt', with *will* as the emergent virtue in the young child. A third challenge, as we have just seen with our friend Angus, is 'initiative versus guilt', leading on to strength of *purpose*. Trained as a child analyst after a difficult early life and adoption by a paediatrician, Erik Erikson had initially conceptualised these as preschool challenges, initially within the mother–child bond and extending to family life, with his fourth challenge of 'industry versus inferiority' relating to early school life and the developing virtue of *competence*.

The Eriksons' 'stages' as challenges in real lives

The Eriksons' thinking has been helpfully reviewed, expanded and illustrated for us by Donald Capps, an American theologian, who through story brings the theoretical ideas to life.[16] Capps makes a cogent case for the Eriksons' first four challenges being effectively faced in our first four *decades*, reinforcing the points that the timing of acquisition of these virtues is less important than our belief in their relevance, and that they constitute a story containing useful truths about life. Capps moves many of the Eriksons' acquisitions of 'virtue' (such as those of *caring*, *loving* and *wisdom*) away from early life through to our later decades, giving us vivid, real-life vignettes or case histories from interviews, many derived directly from the Eriksons' own lifetimes of collaborative research work. The vignettes provide both hope and encouragement for readers in the difficult midlife period: they illuminate real-life dilemmas which must somehow be resolved by the participants – many involve the care of elders.

This testimony from Erikson's clinical practice and findings, and the pastoral encounters described by Capps, bring new urgency to our own reconsideration of purpose in later life. Capps boldly and believably reassigns the Eriksons' four challenges of *identity versus identity confusion*, *intimacy versus isolation*, *generativity versus stagnation* and *integrity versus despair or disgust* to life beyond 50, a clarification which the Eriksons themselves acknowledged in their later publications.

Let's bear in mind as we go on that the respective four virtues, falling out as character products of the successful meeting of these late life challenges, according to the Eriksons, were *fidelity*, *love*, *care* and *wisdom*. These will be familiar entities for consideration in any faith group.

Pole 1	Pole 2	Virtue to be explored
Identity	Identity confusion	Fidelity
Intimacy	Isolation	Love
Generativity	Stagnation	Care
Integrity	Despair	Wisdom

Table 1 The four challenging polarities offering grounding for virtue in later life

As Capps has shown us, there is significant latitude about our placement of the successful addressing of challenges and the subsequent acquisition of virtue in any one life. The frequency of citation of the Eriksons' work alone, in the broad sweep of contemporary educational and psychological literature, tells us that their ideas have validity and strike a chord with many. This could be argued to confirm the universality of their applicability and perhaps acquisition of *virtue generally* as *the* fundamental human challenge. Virtues might be just what we need if we are to be able to love our neighbour as ourselves: these ideas seem resonant with our own experiences and so, once understood, can probably usefully apply to those around us whom we encounter, including the older people for whom we might care. It is also the case that any kind of list is open to abuse: it can be used mistakenly as something that *must be achieved*, rather than as an open-ended description of possibilities – or, worse, as a stick to be used by the judgemental in meting out punishment. But, health warnings apart, this idea of working with the challenges of a *stage* of life, which then results in some further character development and moral robustness, is at the heart of the Erikson model: their big idea. This makes sense to us: we learn, through challenging the difficulties presented to us, how we would *like* to behave and how we and others *actually* behave: the important thing remains that we *learn*.

Challenges for Angus and Josephine

So, at some time in each of their long lives, Angus and Josephine will have wrestled with these challenges. We might wonder, for instance, about Esme and Bill (Angus' parents) in their young adulthoods, raising their young boy, and whether for example it was difficult for an infant Angus to develop trust in his mother, with her having little initial family support, being so far from home and being a threat, a competitor for resources and food. Angus would seem, at least on the surface, to have got on just fine with this and with other early life challenges. But developmental life is complex: while the virtues of *hope*, *will*, *purpose* and *competence* seem to have emerged well enough for both Angus and Josephine despite their circumstantial differences, one can already see from their respective stories the way in which different opportunities could impact on the personal development of these individuals, who already of course carry different genetic and early environmental influences and effects.

Let's take, for further illustration, an example of Angus, the boy of eight, starting out at his public preparatory school, unconsciously wrestling with Erikson's polar challenge of *industry versus inferiority*. Angus meets both poles of this dilemma, oscillating between the sheer pleasure and motivating forces of well-intentioned teaching driving him towards developing an *industrious* self, and the demotivating effects of bullying and peer pressure to oppose the academic values of the school as an *inferior* self. Only when this battle has played itself out in terms of the development of a consistent pattern of behaviour on Angus' part could we reasonably say that he has begun to exhibit *competence* as Erikson meant it, and thereby to be ready for the later challenge of *intimacy*.

This process might take months or years, and might (as Capps would have it) only come into focus at a much later life stage. The Eriksons eventually described up to nine challenges, depending on which version of their published work is consulted. Facetiously, one wonders perhaps, if they had lived even longer, beyond their 90s, whether they might eventually simply have concluded that each day presented its own challenges and stopped writing.

Although the emphasis of their great legacy is on child development, our emphasis here is on later lives, our own and those for whom we care. We might usefully focus briefly on just one more such later-life challenge. Josephine, single, in her early 60s and retired from her lifetime of missionary work overseas, has returned to village life in the south of England. It's no surprise that her English social network, such as it is after many years abroad, is based on the church community where she lives. Josephine has been an assertive (*competent, industrious*) individual, exhibiting leadership in a variety of African communities, working with various charities; she is finding it difficult to adjust to being 'an ordinary parishioner' with no leadership role. One challenge for her, identified by Erikson but located in the seventh decade by Capps, is now to deal with *generativity versus stagnation*. In other words, can she find a new role for herself, wherein she might put her skills and talents to good use, enthusing and motivating others, or is she destined for fruitless struggle and stagnation, for failure to carve a niche for herself? Can she adapt to this major change in her later life, continuing to grow without bitterness? Depending on the outcome of this struggle, Josephine may become an individual who effectively cares for herself and her community, perhaps using the opportunities of shared worship and the tools she has developed of contemplation and prayer, and giving spiritual, prayer-based (rather than practical) hands–on care. Without real mastery of herself in this challenge, she might well become an embittered and isolated elder, setting herself up for a future of despair. There are issues for us here which are further teased out in a later chapter on retirement.

These are complex psychological issues; again, we do well to understand them in ourselves and our own situations, before projecting ourselves and our own blind spots into the care of our fellows. So, as the airline cabin staff tell us, 'Apply your own oxygen mask before attempting to assist others.'

The acquisition of virtue: implications for ageing

As we have hinted, there may be painful personal issues awakened here, within the mysteries of human psychology, and as we think of our own 'wrestling': a hymn from time immemorial reminds us, 'Dark the path that lies behind us, strewn with wrecks and stained with blood'.[17] In real life, one in four of us will experience major mental disorder at some point. Some of us do need and seek psychological help. These life challenges are not easily met and overcome, at least not fully, nor will we all acquire all possible virtue, at least not quickly, nor even necessarily in this lifetime. And we can take comfort from an absence of evidence that the authors believed that these challenges needed to be met in *order*, or that the virtues were necessarily to be *hierarchically* acquired. It's interesting that *fidelity*, *love* and *care* are virtues mentioned quite late in the story, when they are so obviously salient to the *early* life of the child in the arms of the mother, and it does make us wonder both about the essential circularity of developmental life and about current societal wisdom with its focus on work rather than on maternal nurture. Sue Gerhardt's second major work has more on this particular topic.[18]

While we can't expect of ourselves that we will instantly be virtuous, we are taught and expected as Christians to *hope*. It's interesting to wonder, in the light of work by Erikson and others, just how much of our capacity for hope relates to our early life and mothering, and how much to later life experience. Erikson's virtues of *will*, *purpose*, *competence* and *fidelity* are seen from a slightly different perspective from those in traditional Christian literature, but relate well to what an earlier era called *fortitude*, *prudence*, *chastity* and *temperance*; *love*, *care* and *wisdom*. These virtues, perhaps most clearly explored in C.S. Lewis' *Mere Christianity*, surely speak to us of how we would want ultimately to be. Lewis tells us of virtue:

> If people have not got at least the beginnings of these qualities inside them, then no possible external conditions could make a Heaven for them – that is, could make them happy with the deep, strong unshakeable kind of happiness God intends for us.[19]

As we age, some of us will inevitably need some form of care, and some of us will become carers. As we said in the introduction, this book is aimed at people who are ageing and people who are caring for those who are ageing: this often proves to be one and the same person! The over-50s are the group most likely to be offering care to their increasingly long-lived parents and other elderly relatives as well as to the younger generation in terms of grandparenting and financial help: the phenomenon of the 'sandwich generation' has been much reported,[20] and describes the position of those moving into the second half of life who are caring both for young children (often grandchildren) and for their increasingly frail elderly relatives. There is an emphasis on the inequality of resource exchange in this relationship and the over-representation of middle-aged women in this category.

In order that we may *be* the help that we want to be to the older generation, we need to think about our own ageing. We also need to try to understand what we might mean by ageing, before we rush to try to help the aged. The better we do this, the better sorted our ideas will be about ourselves and the systems and structures within which we function, and the better will be the outcomes for those whom we try to help, in this 'fullness' of our years.

Again, C.S. Lewis warns us of the hidden dangers of misguided help, this time in *The Screwtape Letters*. Writing of the overbearing compassionate type, he characterises thus: 'She's the kind of woman who lives for others. You can tell the others by their hunted expression.'[21] There is obviously a two-way relationship between carers and cared-for, each able to help the other in different ways. So, whether as carers or those cared for, we want to try to be truly helpful to others, to free others from age-associated constraints where possible, to retain and support the gift of choice and not to force into place additional controls or restrictions which result from *our* fear and anxiety. Freedom to choose and to be oneself is an enduring value: in the giving of care from a position of relative strength, we want to empower others, rather than to be or, perhaps worse, to posture as powerful ourselves. In the receiving of care needed because of difficulties of ageing, we want to be gracious but to retain as much choice as possible, in an imperfect situation. Ageing, we suggest, can be a process of awakening to complexity, *at the same time* as it is a pursuit of simplicity.

The passage of time: the inescapable journey

Ageing, the *Collins English Dictionary* tells us simply, is 'the process of growing old', implying a passage from conception to death through a lifetime or span. We are trying to see beyond the idea that ageing is just about decline, skin wrinkles, hair loss and painful joints. Of course, these come with the ageing territory as often do many degenerative disorders. Nor is ageing just about a time of life when those whom we love get ill and sometimes die – tragic though this may be. Ageing, whatever else it is about, must be about changing and deepening our understanding of our place, in and outside time, which as we all know can be a struggle. The journey into old age gives us the opportunity to deepen our faith and relationship with God through awakening our senses and simplifying our lives. This is what we would say ageing is *for*. It is a blessing, a privilege and a responsibility.

Simply being

Think for a moment about a beautiful sunset. In truth, of course, it isn't a 'sunset' at all, but represents the phenomenon of our earthly home planet passing the sun at some velocity, turning its face instead towards the sun's other millions of galactic neighbours. Gravity holds us, perhaps kindly, as we watch. We stand, still in reverie but perhaps slowly awakening, still thinking about the beauty of the reds and golds which speed around, still rotating on our earthly axis, backwards, away towards tomorrow as both time and space pass us. We are out of our own control, and in orbit around a flaming, explosive ball of gas on which we are totally dependent for heat and light, for our lives in fact, and yet which is slowly cooling. These thoughts, despite their basis in reality, may terrify some. As we enjoy the sunset and the evening air, as we literally and perceptibly 'take them in', we might also remember that we are enveloped in an atmosphere increasingly composed of toxic gases including carbon dioxide and various nitrogenous derivatives and which only intensifies the beautiful colours that we witness. Here we are, in space: that space includes the psychological space within us, in which all our considerations of this chapter belong. And, while the toxic may appear beautiful, it tragically does not stop being toxic: another powerful reminder for later life. Meanwhile, we 'keep watch'.

The 'complexification' of life leads to simplicity

Perhaps, then, however reluctantly, we can acknowledge that things are not as simple as we have sometimes allowed them to seem to us. And, while we are in the process of awakening, of getting things into proper proportion and perception, let's also incorporate into our thinking the increasingly coherent argument offered by contemporary physicists, that time does not exist independently of space, and that therefore we can no longer reasonably see time as simply linear. We need to think about space too, including the space we allow inside ourselves for that thinking and reflecting: *psychological space*. These sorts of thoughts and the issues touched upon in this chapter can be a real struggle.

Challenging the modern secular idea that ageing is essentially decline, followed by death, is increasingly countercultural work. But our journey into ageing encourages us to think differently and to see our life in the world as both deeply complex and cruel, both loving and kind given our cultural heritage, both toxic and healing, both finite and infinite given the modern science. We don't need to give up the pleasure we experienced at the sunset just because there are violent but distant reactions and explosions taking place. The sunset is still beautiful, and so is the complexity that gives us the sunset. Awakening to the idea of paradox allows us to glory in complexity, at the same time as simply gazing in wonder at beauty. And our new approach of deeper thought might give us fresh hope for our lives, particularly if, in retrospect, we have some sense that we might have been wasting any of our time rotating hopelessly and helplessly towards tomorrow. With Erikson and others, we can see this as developmental necessity, an investment.

Given the space–time realities in which we find ourselves, in which both pass, and in which we struggle onwards, we are right to ask, 'What is ageing for?' Probably, like the cooling sun, we want to be able to conserve our energies, our strengths, and to use and invest these wisely. What might we find space for in life, if we really think about it? What might we choose?

What doesn't kill you makes you stronger

Our ageing is defined by being time-based, and about being awake to the realities, however hazardous. It is also, given the time-honoured golden rule of 'do as you would be done by', about how we might help, or, more fundamentally, how we *relate to*, others. It's something to do with our strength (or virtue) and about the application of human energies, something about what space we might occupy, something about how we might conduct ourselves, and it's also about discovering *who* we might want to be (or who we are). A detailed philosophical discussion of the physics or science behind these ideas about time and its passage is not our focus here, but we recommend Carlo Rovelli as a good start.[22] We can reasonably gloss over the epistemological and ontological issues, but we cannot avoid one vital question: if time isn't linear, if its passing doesn't just equate to my getting older, then what is the purpose of my span? And what should I be doing with it. *What is my life for?*

Many of us, despite the metaphysical hazards, have got at least that far. Taking now a specifically religious tack, a familiar answer could be: 'To love the Lord my God with all my heart, soul, mind and strength: and to love my neighbour as myself'. That will make us think about love. And we might also usefully remember that we are the ones doing the whizzing about in space: none of it is revolving around *us*. So, in answering the vital question, we might add the rider, 'Yes, and not to be fretting so much about those wrinkles, hair loss and joint pains, either!' Therein lies the challenge: one vision of ageing might not be the answer for everyone, and we do have to contend with the struggles and realities of illness, our own and those of others. But the equating of ageing with illness, whether we contort ourselves by fruitless attempts to divide this into categories of 'physical' or 'mental', is a diversion leading (in this universe at any rate) to a cul de sac, to a black hole, to nowhere.

We hope we leave a sense in this chapter, beyond the paradox, of the strengthening impact on each of us of *experience* (events that change our ways through struggle), something about human development in respect of its challenges, our struggles, the virtues we might want to develop, and something of how the challenges we face help to develop those virtues. Such understandings will prove indispensable if we are to really help others with their ageing and to avoid simply being patronising. We'll be tackling this in a reassuringly linear, but hopefully also interesting way regarding human development, maturation, love *and purpose* because, however much of a struggle it seems, these are the bits about ageing we find interesting and vital.

Conclusion

We might, then, dare to hope that in consequence of our faith practice, as the result of relatively detached study of human development, or simply by dint of survival of the 'slings and arrows of outrageous fortune', by our survival of the refiner's fire of everyday life, we can acquire some positive, valuable and stable character traits. This will hopefully make us virtuous, literally strong people, capable of withstanding the diabolical forces of this world and arguably, as C.S. Lewis again puts it in *Mere Christianity*, making us fit for a world or life beyond this one. Indeed, Lewis argues that without virtue we would never be fit for the life promised through our faith, and that it is our life's task therefore to become virtuous. However flawed we are, however the moment finds us, we are charged with being in relation with our neighbour; however the neighbour's needs are expressed, however dependent they may seem, we must respond lovingly, or as Jesus said:

> Things that make people fall into sin are bound to happen, but how terrible for the one who makes them happen! It would be better for him if a large millstone were tied around his neck and he were thrown into the sea than for him to cause one of these little ones to sin. So watch what you do!
> LUKE 17:1–3

Now there is a challenge: we need to get that oxygen mask on ourselves first, even if it's hard to fasten.

We are making an active choice here to see ageing as the opportunity of a journey towards and with God. Our individual journeys always offer us the chance, through valid personal struggle, to acquire personal strengths or virtues. It is the acquisition of such virtues that constitutes life's purpose, and makes us of use to others. We have affirmed that this journey of acquisition of virtues, or maturation, offers opportunity to 'do as you would be done by', to respect, cherish and love others, as one indeed should do in relation to oneself. Of course, we all must, to the varying extents imposed by chance, cope with the slings and arrows that life sends. We must find compassion for others in their struggles. Many of the struggles we see around us, even into later adulthood, struggles with substance misuse or with depression, struggles with difficult family relationships, have their roots in early maternal attachment difficulties or parenting styles.

We have reported here something of the currently accepted biological understandings of love and nurture, and something of the enduring analytic ideas on human psychological development. We have touched on a few of the struggles in the lives of Angus and Josephine, which continue, in their complexity, into later chapters, illustrating something of life's challenges and opportunities for virtuous strengthening. We have pointed the interested reader to fuller accounts of these psychological observations. We have largely glossed over the challenges of ontology, religious dogma and molecular biology, although these also touch on the question 'What is ageing?' In the next chapter, we broaden the discussion about 'ageing' away from developmental psychology into the wider sociological literature, where the genesis and implementation of derived political and social policy will have direct implications for Angus and Josephine.

Chapter 3

Successful ageing: the story so far

The closing years of life are like the end of a masquerade party, when the masks are dropped.[23]

I have done my best in the race, I have run the full distance, and I have kept the faith.

2 TIMOTHY 4:7

Introduction

Perhaps, like us, you experience a sense of disquiet visiting older people in hospital, in care homes and alone at home. We are all likely to share an interest and common purpose in caring for our elders, or at least in assisting professional health and social care staff with the provision of that care. Perhaps many of us entertain an idea that things could somehow be better done. We might do well to bear in mind the old medical maxim: '*Primum non nocere*': first, do no harm. The seemingly dry theoretical sociological considerations we outline below have much in common with psychoanalytic understandings: after all the effortful research, and once explained, understood and adopted, they are usually then construed as something of 'common sense', something miraculously known already. Without reference to some underlying structure, however, without an 'anatomy' of ageing if you like, it is all too easy to slip into our own prejudices and taken-for-granted assumptions.

We have introduced Angus and Josephine. They present very different forms of ageing, and different challenges with regard to their spiritual needs and support. No doubt these characters will recall for readers many individuals already met in daily life. We might have our presuppositions as to who is doing better, who worse. In Chapter 2, we investigated what might be *meant* by ageing. We presented the view that ageing is a complex and essentially lifelong process of coming to terms with oneself and one's environment, and a process of making choices to find meaning; we presented the journey as a search for a balance between hope and despair. As Christians charged to love God with all our hearts, souls, minds and strength, and with loving our neighbour as we love ourselves, if we are to have hope of achieving this in *any* way, no matter how briefly or sporadically and no matter with what difficulty, then we are aiming to be 'successful' as people.

We would argue, then, that the successful ager, in every age, is she who manages to navigate a way through the slings and arrows of outrageous fortune, both external and internal, and to find a balance that offers freedom and choice, rather than imprisonment and prescription. This is greatly aided by embarking consciously and purposefully on a journey of the soul or spirit, which at its core contemplates and addresses meaning and purpose. And we might just spell out here the belief that there are slings and arrows of internal psychological fortune and misfortune, capable of casting significant shadow on the journey, as well as external situational and geographical fortunes and misfortunes to which individuals are subject, and which are largely outside our control. We need resilience. We address this a little later.

So, our actual control over our lives is always precarious and often an illusion. As Christians, we are taught this and taught to surrender ourselves to God's love, relinquishing control. In practice, this is a hard thing: our culture has emphasised increasingly in recent times our need to be independent.

When it comes to religious discipline, we focus on the Christian journey of faith, but others will take different spiritual paths that have equal value to them. We argue that the spiritual journey is the main vehicle by which ageing can be made successful *despite* the vicissitudes of ageing, and the forces within and without that influence our individual development. These next three chapters look first at the idea of successful ageing in our Western research-based culture, and then link the possibilities of success to the idea of the spiritual journey.

The spiritual journey

'Spiritual' and 'journey' may be rather overused terms these days but, for all their liberal and somewhat sloppy ubiquity, we think this phrase still provides the best metaphor for an inevitable human search for the meaning of one's self, life and purpose. As we discuss in Chapter 8, this search becomes more pressing in the second half of life. We journey partly alone and partly in relationship with one another, finding meaning through each other by trying to love each other as Christ intended. As we journey we age, and the meaning and experience of our ageing are informed by our choice of spiritual journey. We would say that we are all on a spiritual journey, no matter how unclear it is to us or others. We would say that life *is* a spiritual journey. Our choice has been to make it a Christian journey and to use our Christian history, heritage and forefathers as our guides via the scriptures and interpretive works. Others will choose different guides. If the spiritual journey is our primary task, then it becomes more pressing and vital as we age that we self-consciously engage in the journey and that we can connect with people who can help us with it.

Common definitions of successful ageing

The reason we are concentrating on the idea of *successful* ageing here is partly that this is the term used in a variety of influential studies about ageing in the 'health and social care' field, and this book is particularly aimed at people who are involved in the care of older people, often in these settings. We can usefully bring this research to bear here to shine a light: extending the metaphor of journey, we can hopefully save ourselves, using existing research evidence, from going off on unhelpful diversions. Generally, we do have in our culture received ideas of what 'successful ageing' might be, and these personal and professional preconceptions can influence the way in which we think about the people we care for, and how we think of our own impending ageing. We have in our mind's eye the archetypal 'successful' ager. We believe it to be important that we look at this carefully, before we start offering spiritual care and support to older people.

The term 'successful' is contentious, insofar as it implies that there is something called 'unsuccessful' ageing, which, as we shall see, is contested by sociologists and gerontologists, and contributes to an ageist approach to the second half of life. More of that later.

Summary of successful ageing criteria

In the following table, we have summarised the kinds of attributes, ideas and theories that are understood to indicate successful ageing. These ideas come from both empirical research and the *vox populi*, evident in most journalistic endeavours on most days. It will not be lost on you that most of the criteria listed below could equally well apply to all age groups! One person's theory is another's prescription or direction for good practice. The work on successful ageing is a mixture of both theory and prescription.

Research-based understanding of successful ageing	*vox populi* interpretation
Longevity	Living longer than the previous generation – generally living longer is an achievement. Living into the ninth and tenth decade becomes 'normal'.

Good health	Maintaining *good* health assumes that *good* is being able to function independently without formal help into old age. Independence in carrying out activities of daily living, being able to extend the midlife health and capacity into older age.
Financially secure and comfortable	Having enough income through pensions (state and other) and savings; to be able to live a life which involves some treats and extras; to be able to maintain a pleasant living environment. Assumes that money is inherently a *good*. To have something to pass on to children or other family members.
Possession of all faculties	Being cognitively intact and being able to make decisions and retain control over oneself and one's life; not having dementia or related cognitive impairment; being able to see, hear, smell, taste and touch, enough for a continued quality of life to be experienced. Being treated as a fully functioning human being.
Ability to compromise, compensate and adapt	Being flexible and thinking ahead. Not being rigid and unable to anticipate problems. Being able to make sensible compromises and adapt to changing abilities by enhancing what can be enhanced. Assumption of endless human flexibility, changing ethics based on shifting philosophies. Assumption of managing pace of change.
Occupation	Being involved in worldly activities, and being able to occupy oneself in what feels like a useful way. Having things to do that are considered worthwhile. Enjoying one's own life and being interested in the lives of others.
Productivity	Still earning a living, or being able to look after oneself financially. Being seen to contribute to society despite one's advancing years.
Scope for selective disengagement	Having capacity to choose what one continues to do and what one modifies or stops doing.
Social networks	Having access to groups of people who are like-minded and doing things that are enjoyable together. Seeing oneself as part of a group or part of several groups.
Confiding relationships	Having relationships with others (often family) that are meaningful and fruitful. Having people to talk to and trust. Being in relationships with others that give one a sense of equality and mutual exchange.
Connectivity	Feeling part of something bigger. Not feeling isolated and alone. Seeing a bigger picture. Being connected to others and to other ideas. Being part of the world, maintaining an interest in the world. Acknowledging some spiritual overview.
Lifelong learning	Continuing to learn and grow.

Table 2 Interpretations of 'successful ageing'

Link between successful ageing and spiritual journey

Ageing is not confined to the old, as we have seen in Chapter 2. We are all ageing, all the time; the interest comes when the journey gets turbulent, and when self-regulation as a coping mechanism doesn't seem enough. The imperative of reconciliation and integration as described by the Eriksons[24] may be more pressing in old age, but it nevertheless speaks to us all. We are all ageing whatever age we happen to be; we are all spiritual beings and we are generally all trying to be successful, integrated, reconciled individuals. Ageing and spirituality are relevant to every individual. Successful ageing, as we can see from the table above, is concerned with the 'successful self'.

The nature of theories

Gerontology, the study of ageing, is multidisciplinary, aimed at understanding the ageing process and at encompassing ideas within sociology, psychology and medicine, nursing, geography, economics and politics. Consequently, there are a variety of models and 'theories' about successful ageing. A theory should identify, explain and predict behaviour for us; and a theory of successful ageing should be able to identify it, to explain why successful ageing is present or absent in each group, and to predict the circumstances in which successful ageing will occur. This, then, will lead us to successful ageing promotion strategies, predicted from the theory. It also should have power to offer us templates for good care. However, this theory can sometimes be presented as a way we *should* be or *ought to* be, rather than how we find things to be: much depends on the nature of the research that underpins the 'theories', and on the perspective of those doing the research. Empirical work is always flawed and influenced by assumptions and expectations; theories of ageing are no exception. This book is not about research methods, but the reader should be aware that there is important debate about the nature of what constitutes 'good' method in social and healthcare research, and about what constitutes valid and reliable research findings.

Early theories of successful ageing that have become part of everyday thinking

Disengagement or activity

Cumming and Henry, American gerontologists writing in the 1960s, presented a model of 'desirable' ageing, which involved the disengagement or withdrawal of the older person from mainstream society.[25] This empirically-based theory suggested that there was a natural and efficacious withdrawal of the older person from mainstream society. In this model, clinging on to middle-aged norms and roles was inappropriate and unhelpful to social cohesion. Our Angus may have done this by retiring from work, but arguably hasn't done so if he is fiercely insistent on visiting the golf club three times per week, reinforcing it as a mental obsession! Cumming and Henry's argument was that there is and *should be* an age-related functional withdrawal that allows for the smooth transition of roles from one generation to another. In this theory, 'success' is understood to be in terms of the degree of smoothness of the handing over of power from one generation to the next. This theory was not well received by those who preferred, as they saw it, a more active and positive approach to ageing.

In the ensuing competition between disengagement and activity for theories of ageing, we can see how theories also become prescriptions, requirements and politically laden. The impact of theory on current service philosophy and provision almost certainly means that Angus is much less of a worry to a primary care team and GP than Josephine, whereas a community mental health team might be more worried about Angus. While the activity theorists won the day in the 60s, it is sobering to see a range of disengagement-type theories now offered across the media. The envy and annoyance at the baby-boomer generation, who are now in their 60s and 70s, comes with the suggestion that many of the economic difficulties of the younger generation are a consequence of the profligacy and irresponsible behaviour of their immediate elders. One wonders what pressures this confers on relationships between Angus and his grandchildren? Older people are adversely affecting the lives of younger people, so the argument goes. This has a certain biblical familiarity to it: the prodigal son required his inheritance to live his life unfettered by his father's wishes. His father complied, and could thereafter only wait in hope of reconciliation in the face of the folly of youth. Samuel's sons and elders came to him to point out that he was old, and that 'people no longer walked in his ways'. They asked for a king who would lead them into *glory*, rather than an old prophet who seemed to them out of touch. We return to this familiar and crucial issue later.

Extending midlife

There are several other overlapping models or theories of successful ageing, which share some basic ideas about the presence of good health, independence and social activity, and the absence of overwhelming need or disease.

Rowe and Kahn offer us a model that strongly equates success with good health, via the absence of chronic disease, the presence of fitness and the ability to perform physical functions.[26] Implicit in this model is that longevity is an achievement, and that compression of morbidity is a goal. Compression of morbidity means that there is a long and relatively healthy life which only starts to deteriorate at the very end of the lifespan, rather than extended ill health and disability. But, we might ask, does this approach allow us to see Angus as healthy if it pays no attention to his depressions of mood, anxiety or panic attacks?

Baltes and Baltes consider a behaviour-related model of adaptation and compensation.[27] They offer seven propositions that comprise known factors associated with ageing, for instance changes *in use* of memory, and this leads them to suggest that successful ageing is a process of selection, optimisation and compensation. The successful ageing process is one that finds a balance between changing abilities that keeps an equilibrium which can maintain independent living. If these balances and adjustments can be made, then the older person can maximise their 'efficiency' in terms of conducting a normal and 'mainstream' life. They do not mention the spiritual specifically. However, they do very helpfully point out that the task of selection, compensation and optimisation is not confined to the old. Losses and gains are a feature of every decision and they discuss briefly the use of dependence as part of the adaptive process. This lets us think about Josephine, her intention and will to adhere to a prayer routine, and the need for health and care staff to respect and operate around this. What happens to Josephine's 'health' when services are so stretched that they lose this 'slack'?

Developmental theories of ageing

We have already discussed the developmental and psychological theories or models, particularly those of the Eriksons and Donald Capps, who developed the idea that people move through psychological stages linked to opportunities to develop virtues. These stages are vital for their journey of personal development. Later stages may be related to reconciliation. Antonovsky also pursued the idea of a sense of coherence being a state of spirit that allowed one to feel content, and to understand one's meaning and place in the world.[28] This is a very 'internal' psychological idea that reminds us of Josephine. Antonovsky looked at this in relation to how people perceived their health, and remained 'healthy' (or perhaps just 'not needy') despite medical ill health. The individual's way of understanding themselves in the world influences their understanding of illness and wellness.

All these models assume a *movement* along life's journey. Successful movement within old age is, to some extent, defined by the degree to which these changes can be noiseless and untroubling to other members of society, including family members. Being 'great for one's age' is almost always associated with being untroubling to others. It is once old age starts being a nuisance and disrupting other parts of social life that it becomes a focus for concern: perhaps when Angus' daughter can't get him to come to a party, or when Josephine's visitors complain to the district nurse about the smell in her house?

A common story about a 'successful' older person is often implicitly underpinned by the idea that he or she does what they are told, and cheerfully! Despite the popularity and intuitive appeal of Jenny Joseph's poem 'When I grow old I shall wear purple', where she declares an intention to behave badly and break the rules, the reality is that conforming and fitting in to societal expectations is greatly encouraged over being 'unusual' and therefore potentially demanding. Conformity has a tendency to make a majority feel safer and better. The clamour regarding the apparent rise in the prevalence of dementia alongside an increase in longevity, and regarding the concurrent increase in 'young older' people looking after their older parents, has become deafening in our media, and is increasingly a subject for discussion and, seemingly, anguish. It seems to matter less whether the path of disengagement and withdrawal, or of insistent active engagement, is taken. More attention is paid to the degree to which these processes are inconvenient and troubling to general social life.

ANGUS and **JOSEPHINE's** successful ageing stories

Angus is a fit 82-year-old. He can drive and has a comfortable car. He is well off in relative terms and can afford cruises and holidays. His story is one of playing golf three times a week with friends of his own age. He attends his local church regularly and is an active member of the congregation. He has a big garden, which he enjoys, and he is very sociable. He is always ready for a party. The local community in which he lives is very supportive of him and he has numerous old and established friends with whom he spends his time. His wife of 50 years died two years ago, when he was 80. He goes to a bereavement group set up by the hospice. It is when he is alone that he finds it difficult to motivate himself to do anything. When one gets down to the detail below the broad-brush strokes of the picture painted, he seems to look to others to act as a stimulus for his activities. He feels that his home is somehow depleted, and he is not sure where home is any more. Is Angus a successful ager? He is certainly medically healthy relative to his peers, and he has money and friendships. But he is desperately lonely, and without continued external stimuli he becomes very depressed.

Josephine is medically unfit. She is 96. She lives alone and is completely housebound. She can't walk. She can't go out. She can't see. She has increasing urinary problems that alarm her, and now she deals with them herself rather than declare them. She has little money. Her neighbours are very kind and she has many visitors. She has a care manager, whom she pays, and who does a variety of tasks for her, including her correspondence. She fears being 'taken away' into residential care. She resists being admitted into hospital, and these fears make her even less mobile. Her surroundings are not very clean. She has cats that she leaves food for, and she puts out food for the mice that come in from the unkempt garden space.

She has a very clear and prayerful daily routine. She wakes at five o'clock in the morning and prays as part of a remote prayer network. She also has a prayer and meditation time at four o'clock in the afternoon. She never misses these, and asks her visitors to call at times that do not disrupt this. She sees her community role as bound up with her ability to pray and intercede on behalf of others. This is a lifelong view. Her visitors bring her news from the outside, and she asks intelligent and searching questions about this news. She constructs her prayers accordingly. Her cognitive abilities are intact, and she says that her meditational life keeps her mentally sharp despite her great age. If she misses her prayer times for some reason, she reports becoming disorientated. She fears admission into a residential or nursing home, knowing that she will not be easily able to maintain her personal routines.

Considering these two elders in the context of the theories, models, prescriptions and opinions offered by gerontology and society on successful ageing, it may be difficult to allocate the label 'successful ageing' to one and not the other, without imposing our personal values on them. Angus, on the face of it, has a healthy lifestyle, little illness or symptoms and is active and well off. Josephine is housebound, and is quietly becoming a heavy community care user and a potential 'problem', in respect of her wishes and needs being at odds with the requirements of the health and social care services to 'manage risk' and meet current standards of safety and cleanliness. Now, neither Angus nor Josephine is noisy, and neither is intentionally a nuisance. Pursuing the idea that our current social understanding of 'successful ageing' is dangerously close to being that of 'not becoming a nuisance to others', what might be said of Angus when he finds himself unable to rouse himself from his apathy or depression? His chosen lifestyle cannot tolerate withdrawal of social stimuli. Angus may become withdrawn from his lunch invitations, and not wish to play golf with his pals. If the situation with neighbours and friends changes, he may find himself in real difficulties. And Josephine's chosen lifestyle will put her increasingly 'at risk'. If Josephine falls and breaks her leg she will be hospitalised and, in all likelihood, will not come back to her house, which in any case requires the attention of environmental services.

Implications of successful ageing theories for real-life practice

We can see that 'success' is quite a complex thing to define, and not the 'obvious' idea we might earlier have had in mind. Is Josephine less successful because she is physically disabled, is housebound and is imprisoned in her failing body? Or is Angus less successful because he is only able to function when others are around, and has fearful doubts about his personal meaning and purpose? Who decides what successful ageing is, and what criteria can be used?

These are philosophical, political and economic questions, as well as social ones, and might ultimately become legal ones, when the ability of individuals to make informed decisions is called into question. Decisions at the end of life about active treatment or passive care are inevitable, no matter who is ultimately called upon or legally authorised to make them, and they inform our own prejudices and opinions that lurk just under the surface in our understanding of ageing.

Defining successful ageing is a dangerous and incomplete activity. However, it happens implicitly all the time, and we do well to think about it in some detail, if we are sensibly to examine our own ageing and to work effectively with elders. If we have in our minds an idea of a successful ageing process (which, of course, we all do), then how can we behave and relate to people who, in our view, are not ageing well and successfully? How do we adapt our own behaviour to age as well as we can by our *own* criteria? Those people who extol the virtues of living life at full pace despite increasing age, and who maintain their youthful stances in the face of old age, will presumably feel that failure to maintain that pace is a mark of lack of success. If someone of 80 years of age can run marathons for charity, but his neighbour cannot or does not choose to, does this mean that the neighbour is less successful? Many of us tend to objectify our ageing, and to perceive ageing in rather black-and-white terms, which takes us right back to Melanie Klein's challenge of psychological maturation: for me to be ageing well and successfully, others must be ageing less well and less successfully.

A different approach to successful ageing

To recap, there are broadly two types of theory of successful ageing. These two 'theories' or approaches of 'disengagement' and 'activity' have dominated the research and practice agenda in the decades since the 1960s. The initial feeling of horror about disengagement (and its being a bad thing for successful ageing) has more recently been revisited in relation to spiritual development, and 'a bit of disengagement' is now thought to be an aid to spiritual development. Indeed, 'gerotranscendence' is the idea that older people start to re-view their worlds and reconstruct that which is important to them.[29] This is not a million miles away from disengagement and re-engagement in more spiritual matters. More of this later, in Chapter 8.

Some 20 years ago, when we were both working in a medical school, we conducted an informal study which somewhat reinforces the positive ideas contained within partial or selective disengagement. This study was called 'Asking the experts: Ageing, the journey of a lifetime' and involved interviewing at length 16 older people, most in their ninth decade, most of whom considered themselves, and were considered by others, to be experts on ageing. These people rightly all considered themselves to have in-depth knowledge of gerontological literature. A striking finding was their almost universal acceptance that they would, did and intended to continue to disengage from some aspects of their earlier lives. They practised what they called 'partial' disengagement. They declared a willingness, indeed a necessity, to disengage from some aspects of their lives to preserve others, confirming Baltes and Baltes' work on optimisation, selection and adaptation.[30] Disengagement from big, high-profile positions in society was sometimes a painful necessity. We discuss the whole area of ageing as a management of change process in Chapter 9, covering retirement. Very few of the respondents in these interviews were declaring themselves to be actively and fully engaged in their previous professional lives, and neither did they wish or intend to be. For them, life was all about finding a balance, and choosing their engagements and activities. Freedom to choose was of prime importance.

Successful ageing is part of the journey towards successful self

The implication of this study, and of many similar studies looking at the spiritual aspects of ageing, is that the experience of successful ageing should be seen as part of the journey towards the successful self, as defined by achieving an interest in *growing spiritually*. However, mechanisms within society arguably militate against success in this sense. The demand seems to be either that older people should be actively engaged in social life and behaving like younger people, or that older people cannot grasp and manage the complexities of modern life, and should step out and allow themselves to be sidelined (and perhaps patronised). Either way, we may be setting up older people for failure, as the characteristics of what is understood currently to form a 'successful' life are systematically withdrawn or withheld from them.

Successful ageing is perhaps better defined by *the degree to which the individual is comfortable with and reconciled to herself, rather than by a society's comfort with the individual*. The powerful capacity of society for controlling and defining the understanding of ageing makes the journey towards a 'successful self' hazardous, particularly in old age when structures of support are withdrawn, and when expectations of particular modes of ageing are imposed.

Longevity: a primary marker of 'success'?

There is no doubt that we are all living longer. If a woman lives to 60 in the UK today she is, on average, likely to live a further 30 years or thereabouts, and for a man the figure is only a little less. Achieving a great age is still noteworthy, but does not seem to hold the mystery and wonder that it did in the past. Hundredth-birthday telegrams from the Queen present a growing administrative burden! Recently, media reports told of a professor in America who as a centenarian was still using his university office daily, arriving by bus from his home. Interestingly, the article focused on the fact that the university wanted him to retire! We hear of nonagenarians embarking on new educational courses, jumping out of planes for charity and generally behaving in ways that refute the idea of the quiet retreat into old age and decrepitude described by Pat Thane,[31] which is the all-pervasive and culturally acknowledged understanding of ageing. We write more about Thane's work in Chapter 5.

In health and social care research terms, the criterion of longevity is an obvious one for successful ageing. If people live longer because of a specific intervention or a lifestyle choice, then they are obviously successful. If a care home keeps people alive through good nutrition, activities and stimulation and careful body care, then this can be described as successful ageing. Imagine a situation where the care home strapline is 'Twilight Homes: Where nobody dies before they reach 90'!

Godly, graceful ageing

It's interesting that the ancients in the scriptures seemed to start their good works at advanced age. J. Gordon Harris, in a very interesting look at the biblical perspective on ageing, refers to a common theology of ageing which has certain specific characteristics.[32] He also notes that finding a theology of ageing within the scriptures is not an easy task; his work contributes to the increasing body of knowledge linking gerontology and religion. Harris' work is very helpful in taking us back to the Bible. He frames his examination of biblical texts about ageing in the context of the nature of God as presented in the Bible. He makes three propositions:

- God is the agent of blessing.
- God is the protector of social structures.
- God is the proponent of justice.

From this framework, he then considers the specific approach to ageing.

- *God is the agent of blessing*: Ageing is a divine blessing, though not without its difficulties. God's blessing is not always comfortable. This implies that ageing is a process of growth towards God, even though the path is difficult and stony. Ageing is part of our life's journey and God blesses us on this journey.

- *God is the protector of social structures*: The social structures of our society in all ages, it seems, should protect the position of the elderly and provide a continuity through life that is orderly and respectful. Older people are presented and treated with respect as part of the good structures of society.

- *God is the proponent of justice*: Sometimes the social structures are unjust. Older people should not be exploited in their diminished status, and they should and will be protected.

These propositions form the basis for considering what the scriptures say about older people. It also helps us think about a biblical context to the nature of successful ageing.

So, successful ageing might be where:

1   The blessings and gifts of God are acknowledged, and used wisely and reverently. This would mean in practice that, as we grow older, we acknowledge God's role both with us and in the world and we learn to be grateful and humble.

2   The social structures of our society are constructed in such a way that makes it possible for older people to live blessed lives, to live as people who are loved by God and to be a blessing for others, using their knowledge and life experience wisely. In practice, this might mean that older people will have the care and attention they need from the different agencies, to be as well as they can be and as fully functioning as they can be, where choice is retained if possible. The older person's role is to help that process by being as adaptive and creative as they can be.

3   Justice is central to decision-making about social and healthcare policies for the aged, and age in turn is a voice for good, which neither discourages nor oppresses the younger generation who, in their turn, will respect and cherish the elders. Justice is where resources are shared proportionately and appropriately.

This version of successful ageing puts the spiritual life and God's all-encompassing grace centre stage.

Successful ageing and resilience

Successful ageing, as we are framing it here, requires a degree of resilience. Again, resilience is a term that is popular among health scientists, and it is perhaps helpful to define it here. We have borrowed heavily from Frankl's understandings of resilience, which he developed during his incarceration in a concentration camp in Germany during World War II.[33] To preserve his own self, he embarked on a study that investigated how some prisoners survived and others did not. Out of this empirical observational work came his thoughts about resilient personalities.

He identified three characteristics associated with a resilient personality. Firstly, the resilient personality will be realistic. This characteristic means that when bad things happen, the person is not completely thrown and astonished. The person will know that sometimes bad things happen to good people, and that there is a need to be realistic about what might or might not happen. In the context of the concentration camp, the realism is about the possibility of being killed. Accepting that this evil is a reality helped people plan how to avoid being rounded up for the gas chambers. In the case of Frankl's study, acknowledging the reality of the situation made management of extreme difficulty slightly easier. This very much applies to old age. We need to be realistic about the possibility of living long lives and being disabled. We need to be realistic about how we are intending to finance our long lives, in the current financial situation in which we find ourselves. We need to be realistic and well-informed about the nature of the care systems on offer in our current society. We need to be realistic about our relationships and family ties, and the mutual support (or otherwise) that they offer. Being realistic about ageing means accepting that it is probably a journey that includes loss, diminishment and dark moments, but that it also offers the opportunity of hope and salvation.

The second characteristic that Frankl identified was that of having a sense of purpose or meaning that is bigger than ourselves. Those who survived the death camps tended to grasp a bigger picture, and had a greater capacity perhaps to locate themselves in the bigger picture. The resilient personality has some internal understanding that the world is bigger than themselves. The degree to which we can think of ourselves as both in control and part of a general flow of history gives us our location in the world, and the meaning we impose upon our existence in the world.

So, within the concentration camps, those who could see the persecution of the Jews and the consequent behaviour of the German Nazis in a historical context were able to understand their own meaning and role better. The persecution was not personal to them, and neither was the decision about their survival. They were caught up in a historical moment. The persecution of the Jews is bigger than one person's actual experience of it. Those who can see that ageing is part of life, and that its vicissitudes are part of the process and of life, can take less personally the difficulties encountered and are perhaps better able to at least understand their own meaning and purpose in the wider context. Christians who have a sense of God, both within and outside themselves, are also able to find solace in the idea that purpose and meaning are connected to the spirit. Corrie ten Boom's extraordinary testimony about her own experiences of being incarcerated in a Nazi camp during the war shows the degree to which she struggled with God's purpose and her own actions.[34] She found great solace, and ultimately freedom, in her belief that God was in charge, rather than the guards and the captors. This 'bigger-picture' approach is akin to the idea of *connectivity* expressed elsewhere.

The third characteristic of resilience is connected to the ability to be creative and adaptive. This is sometimes linked to the French word *bricolage*, which Claude Lévi-Strauss the anthropologist introduced into social science language in his work *The Savage Mind*.[35] This has since been interpreted a number of times and taken on several meanings, but here it is helpful to refer to it as the ability to find new solutions through using existing materials in a creative way. In the camps, the man who picks up a piece of string that he finds on the floor so that later it might be useful for shoelaces, which will prevent him ruining his footwear, is a man who is being creative. This has resonance with the work of Baltes and Baltes described earlier. In common parlance, we can make the best of whatever situation we find ourselves in in the certain knowledge that we are loved by God, and that we have the capacity to love and live as people who are loved by God. This is not in any way to downplay the worries and 'angst' of ageing that most of us experience, but it gives us a framework and a light to follow.

It is no surprise that the broad characteristics that describe successful ageing, particularly those of adaptability, are like those that describe a resilient personality. Helping older people adopt and practise these characteristics is part of spiritual care. This allows people to discuss, develop and practise their ideas of purpose and meaning, and to discuss the realities of their current situation, and the possible futures they might wish for, in a creative and imaginative way.

Summary

We have tried to emphasise the importance of unpacking the ideas and theories behind successful ageing. We have given a version of successful ageing that borrows from Gordon Harris' work on the representation of ageing in the Bible. We would encourage you now to reflect upon your own assumptions about successful ageing, and to think about older people you know and the degree to which these characteristics are relevant.

We now turn to the relationship between successful ageing and the spiritual journey. We have already hinted at this by suggesting that the spiritual journey is increasingly the focus of attention as we age. Finding meaning in our lives and making sense of what has happened becomes an urgent focus, like it or not. This is the spiritual journey. The successful ager is one who willingly embarks upon that journey.

Chapter 4

The spiritual journey: making meaning

Each individual's experience of life is always potentially fresh. Growing – up and old – resembles a continuous journey down a river flowing inexorably toward the sea.[36]

In Chaim Potok's novel *The Chosen*,[37] a young son is questioning his father about why he continues to fight for a cause that puts him in the way of danger. The father replies:

Human beings do not live forever, Reuven. We live less than the time it takes to blink an eye, if we measure our lives against eternity. So, it may be asked what value is there to a human life. There is so much pain in the world. What does it mean to have to suffer so much if our lives are nothing more than the blink of an eye? I learned a long time ago, Reuven, that a blink of an eye in itself is nothing. But the eye that blinks, that is something. A span of life is nothing. But the man who lives that span, he is something. He can fill that tiny span with meaning, so its quality is immeasurable though its quantity may be insignificant. Do you understand what I am saying? A man must fill his life with meaning, meaning is not automatically given to life. It is hard work to fill one's life with meaning. That I do not think you understand yet. A life filled with meaning is worthy of rest. I want to be worthy of rest when I am no longer here.

Here is the essence of the human spiritual journey. This sentiment of searching for meaning is found in all forms of creative work.

Introduction

We have, we hope, established that ageing is a universal human experience, and it is also uniquely experienced. We all age, we all age differently. This moves us away from the idea of homogeneous groups of 'older people', who can be categorised, stereotyped and collectively 'cared for'. While there are inevitably many shared experiences of ageing, and the process of ageing will carry with it some common markers along the path, the way that we tackle our ageing and the external environmental factors that impact on our ageing will be specific and uniquely experienced. Ageing requires attention to self and the willingness to adapt and change and be accepting of these necessary changes. In this chapter, we come to the heart of the matter. Ageing is a spiritual matter, a spiritual journey. Ageing poses the question: what has my life been about and what does the future hold? Each and every person, whatever their age, is someone on a particular and unique journey through life, which includes self-discovery. Living into old age offers the opportunity to re-explore ourselves, to use our imagination to reconnect creatively with the spiritual energies and natures that are inherent within us. Ageing may be the time for us to rediscover or embark for the first time on journeys of faith. Ageing is a privilege, and our greatest opportunity to grow up and see the world and ourselves afresh.

The spiritual journey

Our journeys through life are usually difficult.[38] Our life journeys are a spiritual matter. Our underlying search for meaning is the basic narrative and interpretive tool we use. The length of our life is infinitesimal in the scheme of things, but the value of the individual living the life is 'something'.

For some of us, religion is the vehicle or mechanism that we will choose by which to live our journey. This is a *theist* route and involves an assumption of God in some form or another. Others will take an a-theist route, one that does not incorporate an assumption of God. Both are spiritual journeys involving the search for meaning and location of self within the world and in relationship to others. Our shared humanity is our spiritual journey. We are all on life's spiritual journey.

ANGUS and JOSEPHINE's spiritual journeys

Let us consider Angus and Josephine again. If we asked Angus directly about his spiritual journey, he would probably look embarrassed and say that he didn't do much of that. He might then volunteer his going to church on a Sunday, being involved in church activities, fundraising and administration, in particular, as his spiritual journey. In truth, his life journey was bound up with his beloved wife who, having died, has left him to travel alone and lonely. He doesn't know how to do this. His church life offers him some practical activities to help him fill his time, but does very little for his ability to reflect and change in the light of new circumstances. His annoyance at the length of the sermons and irritation with the noisy children tend to dominate his impression of church services. His gentle, unproblematic approach to his life has been shattered by the death of his travelling companion. He is lost; he cannot find meaning, except in social activity and the continuation of social manners. He is fearful of being alone, because then the thoughts crowd in and he is overwhelmed by his loss and lost-ness. He has no real basis for a faith that he has adhered to off and on during his 80 years. God is something remote, external and apparently uncaring, almost vengeful, in his mind now. He would probably say none of this and would most certainly tick the box that says 'Church of England' on the census form.

Josephine has now become unable to involve herself in physical communal activity. She cannot go to meetings or raise money through fundraising activities or sponsored walks. She cannot continue her work as verger, opening and shutting the local church and acting as unpaid cleaner. She has learnt over the years and in painstaking ways, through the loss of her fiancé in the war, the distancing from her parents, her isolation as a missionary and now, in her advanced old age, the loss of most of her companions and friends, to look inwards and to rely much more on her internal world. She reads, listens to the radio and receives visits from selected people. She has built up a strong faith in an immanent and present God and, while she no longer attends the church because of her disabilities, she has a strong and vibrant prayer life which is shared with the few remaining lay nuns that she is in touch with by phone. Her prayer calendar, and the contemplation that comes out of that, informs the structure of her day.

Both Angus and Josephine live their lives in relationship to others, as do we all. Angus needs other people to help him function and get through the day. He needs to tell his story. He needs help with reaffirming his status in the community and his value to it, which is bound up with his search for meaning. Josephine also needs other people to help her get through the day. She needs help with bathing, cooking and moving. She is looking for practical help that will keep her at home and allow her to continue her contemplative life as she wishes. Their individual well-being is dependent on others, and that relationship is part of the unfolding of their spiritual journey. Angus, seeing how kind the local community is to him, is buoyed up and encouraged and, as we shall see, begins to formulate different theories about meaning and purpose. Josephine is able to contribute to the spiritual thinking about meaning and purpose of others, those who visit her and those for whom she prays. The relationships are mutual, they are interdependent and they all contribute to the journey of one another.

Spiritual support for Angus and Josephine

What support does Angus look for in his bereaved state? Angus gets his support from his relationships with others, where, in exchange for good manners, charm and good, safe company, he is allowed to tell his stories and rehearse his grief. This is currently his spiritual imperative. Later, he will be able to move on. Now the spiritual caring task required of others by him is to listen, ask questions, be interested, so that he can unfold the loss of his beloved in safety and can begin to accept a future without her presence.

What spiritual support does Josephine look for in her disabled state? Josephine wants to be able to stay in a place where she can continue to feel in control and where she retains choice. This would be a place where she is able to continue to practise her prayer life and reading life. Feeling in control means not being treated as an 'old lady' who is patronised and 'done' to. She has no need to tell her story to her visitors; rather, she tends to listen to theirs and uses what she hears to delve into herself and her reading more thoughtfully. Her needs are quite different from Angus'. Later, they will change again.

Both sets of spiritual needs are valid and important. Both require quite different spiritual care.

The search for meaning

The spiritual journey refers to the search for meaning. What am I, who am I, where did I come from and where am I going? To paraphrase T.S. Eliot's two great questions: 'What is life for and what am I going to do about it?' We consciously and unconsciously search for understanding of ourselves, our own lives.

We have already made reference to Viktor Frankl in Chapter 3. His observations of his fellow prisoners and how they coped with the extreme circumstances in which they found themselves convinced him that mental health and growth depended on finding some meaning and purpose in whatever situation one was in. The discovery of meaning and purpose gave a point to living *and* a method of living. In the concentration camps, although there was an attempt by the Nazis to reduce people to 'mere' numbers, the human spirit that searched for meaning helped the prisoners make sense of what was happening. He noted a variety of responses to incarceration. All illusions (of rescue, fairness, kindness) were destroyed one by one. Normal feelings became abnormal. A lack of emotional response and apathy replaced outrage and fear. Food became the target of all thought and dreams. He also wrote of the point at which people simply gave up the struggle. He wrote movingly of his observations of prisoners who simply would not get up despite beatings and threats and would not eat or move. He was able to predict that they would die within a few days. One confirming sign that they were near to death was when these prisoners smoked their own cigarettes rather than keeping them as vital life-sustaining bargaining chips for extra soup or other bribes. These responses, albeit in very extreme circumstances, are all recognisable in the behaviour of some older people as they become more trapped and ensnared in their bodies, and as they lose control over more and more parts of their lives. This is increasingly the profile of those who live in residential care: as places become scarcer and demand increases, so the disability of the residents increases.

This is sobering stuff. However, Frankl observed the presence of spiritual depths and life. People, even in circumstances of great extremes, drew on memories of love that sustained them. There was an intensification of inner life and an appreciation of beauty. He believed that each individual, no matter how dire their circumstances, had the ability to hold on to a vestige of spiritual freedom, of independence of mind, and could choose his or her attitude in any given set of circumstances. He proposed that the search for meaning took place via:

- Creating a work/doing a deed.
- Encountering someone or something to love and remembering this beloved.
- Rising above oneself – seeing oneself as part of something bigger.

He called these aspects 'tragic optimism'. We think this morphs into the contemporary idea of the resilient personality. He developed his logotherapy further after the war. The data upon which he based his theories provide very extreme examples of humankind's continued and necessary search for meaning, and the sustenance of some kind of spiritual journey despite being subject to barbaric attempts to extinguish the characteristics of living that can be called human.

The spiritual journey refers to the search for the meaning of ourselves, our lives and our understanding of others. Our methods of searching can be seen as spiritual practices, and always involve relationship with others. For many, it involves relationship with God. The spiritual journey is the process and the unfolding of the search. Everybody's search is unique. The spiritual journey is vital to our well-being.

Sometimes the search is obvious and the journey is accepted, understood and embraced. This is the case for Josephine. However, most of the time this search becomes apparent only occasionally; sometimes it is only when difficulties, adversity or great joy, or love assault us that we have moments of realisation of the journey.

The importance of spiritual matters to good health and well-being, is a relationship that is increasingly understood.[39] Ignoring the spiritual core of ourselves leads to discontinuity and distress. This is the case no matter what age you are. In the ageing self, there is a certain urgency about the spiritual aspect. This is perhaps like the urgency that Frankl describes in the concentration camps.

Ageing and the changes that ageing brings, often in sudden disability, chronic decline, loss and grief, provide us with further stimulus to the journey. Ageing is an opportunity for spiritual journey and growth.

Search for meaning in the everyday

A human being interacts with her environment and in so doing searches for, hypothesises and creates meaning. There is meaning and purpose in cooking breakfast, making beds and straightening sheets, walking the dog and ironing clothes, just as there is meaning and purpose in teaching young children, working as a hospital doctor, working in a factory producing equipment, developing computer games and running countries and large businesses. All these acts can be, and are, done in different ways, and each of us makes our own meaning in our own environment. Our daily acts of living provide us with the structure that brings meaning to our lives. There is equally meaning in rest, sleep and inactivity. We are not all great painters, writers or musicians, or politicians or economists. These 'greats' provide us with ideas and food for thought along the way of our journey. This helps us to manage our thinking about meaning. The meaning itself is in our own individual journey.

Telling our stories

From time immemorial, in myths, in fiction, in fairy tales, in factual accounts of lives lived, in scriptures of all kinds, the idea of journey towards a goal that is transformative has been acknowledged and valued. Psychoanalysts draw on the myths and archetypes in their understanding of humankind's journey, and in their attempts to help individuals understand their own journeys. We use these stories to help ourselves understand our own situation more clearly, and as ways to learn. The classic heroic story begins with a naïve but resolute character setting out on a mission to carry out a task that will bring glory and joy to him or her and, importantly, to others. This mission may right wrongs and restore balance. The task will be difficult and dangerous, and many obstacles will put in the way, but the end of the journey will see the return of the hero, changed and reconciled.

This could be a description of the journey of any one of us. The story calls up the archetypes, for example the *hero*. The child leaves the safety of his mother's breast and looks out towards the world, which he knows he must enter. Upon entering it, he finds it to be duplicitous and dangerous. He attempts, with help from loving others, to negotiate his way through the world with many slips on the way; many tricks and traps are laid for him. False love, blind alleys, untruths: he slowly learns to distinguish his own true path from the many closed and dangerous passages he is offered, and he develops the moral core, the spiritual antennae, that will allow him to manage the hazards of life and become a whole person. He returns to his base changed and reconciled, ready to help others. This heroic journey is identifiable everywhere in our thinking, in our art and films and in our books. Most importantly, it is embedded in our assumptions about life.

This classic journey does not tend to include the hazards of ageing and old age, when uncertainty and the uncontrollable increase, and where the comfort of loving supports is stripped away. This bit of the journey tends to be unreported, unless the old man can transform into a younger one as part of the rediscovery.

So, being on a journey, discovering oneself and one's place, is implicit in how we describe and understand ourselves. We tell stories about ourselves all the time. These are always, in a sense, spiritual stories because they involve explaining ourselves and our meaning. We account for how we have got to where we are. This can be from the mundane – how we managed to catch the train despite delays at the station, how we bought ingredients for a meal, only to realise that we didn't have the right pasta, so we had to improvise – to the sublime – how we walked to the station and noticed the beauty of the trees that morning as the sun glanced through them, or how we missed the train because of some drama in the street, which involved us caring for somebody who had fallen. Our stories can be very basic or very convoluted, depending on our character and situation. We explain ourselves through the stories we tell about our journey.

We also rely on other stories about other people to help us understand the world. A good contemporary example is the *Vera* series.[40] This is a TV series based on Ann Cleeves' murder mystery stories. As with most good detective stories, Vera, the senior detective, is a complex character whose personal life journey unfolds in bits and pieces through the series. What we know about Vera in series six is much more than we know in series one. Through each of the episodes, each of which finds Vera trying to resolve a murder, more information comes to light about her own journey, her childhood, her hang-ups, her regrets, the death of her mother as a young girl, the death of her first and perhaps only love, the complicated relationship with her poacher father. We start to wonder why she wanted to be a policewoman, and what it is that makes her so good at solving murders. We are also interested in her interpretations and discoveries of why the murder happened, and the piecing together of other people's stories. The reason that this is so compelling and enjoyable is that we all do it all the time, but, with a fiction series, we can do it in the privacy of our own home. Vera's journey is a journey of searching for meaning. Although she doesn't talk about God or refer to any deep spiritual convictions or indeed doubts, she is nevertheless, and rather reluctantly, searching for herself as she goes about her earthly work, which supports and comforts others.

The soaps are clearly very popular, as are programmes like *The Great British Bake Off*, *Strictly Come Dancing* and *The X Factor*. These long-running programmes have a familiar style and structure and they provide us with stories, with accounts of the journeys of individuals from one place to another; from 'no talent at dancing' to 'winning a dancing competition with the tango': from a 'struggle to bake a cake' to 'winning a cookery competition'. The soap or reality TV characters are earthly and 'like us'; their tragedies and triumphs are recognisable. They have insights and changes of heart; they try to improve themselves or they sink into the grip of badness and malice. We have always told stories and understood each other through the metaphor of story. We are searching for meaning and purpose.

The arc-shaped understanding of life's journey

The Judeo-Christian understanding of life's journey, by which we in the West are all influenced, starts with the arrival of the baby and ends with the decrepit shrivelled old person. Shakespeare's famous lines, spoken by Jacques in *As You Like It*, illustrate this basic Western assumption. The baby mewls and pukes in its mother's arms and the old man retreats 'sans eyes, sans teeth, sans everything'. A gloomy picture, indeed, but one that is seared into our understanding. This is typically represented in a series of pictures of humanity that describe an arc from the infant to the decrepit elder. The apex of this arc is the thrusting middle-aged triumphant person, from which all is downhill. This depiction of life's journey dominates and influences our understanding of ageing. As we shall see later, we make assumptions about diminishment and decrepitude which are in themselves self-fulfilling prophecies. We look for evidence of diminishment in our older folk, and then act on it. We tend to assume decline. Our social and healthcare policies and structures are set up with this arc in mind.

Arduous, heroic and unfulfilled journeys

The scriptures tell us that Moses' life journey was long (he lived to 120). His life was divided into three parts: he started his journey in Egypt, fled to the wilderness, where he lived for another 40 years as a farmer, and then spent the next 40 years returning home. His final days were spent in sight of the holy city, the promised land, but he was still not quite home.

Dante's *Divine Comedy* is possibly the most famous work of fiction, written as a poem around 1320. This three-part piece describes the journey through hell, purgatory and then paradise. He is accompanied by others, the poet Virgil and then his beloved Beatrice. The journey is one of danger and fear, as well as great joy and deepening understanding of self and others. The support he receives on his way, from his companions, sustains and upholds him. This allegory, which tells of the journey of the soul towards God, is deeply moving and highly relevant to our caring for each other and for older people. There may be many aspects of ageing that are difficult, and having good support and companionship along the way can only be a good thing. These common experiences influence our thinking about the Christian spiritual journey.

The Christian spiritual journey

The Christian spiritual journey is particular in its characteristics, namely in relation to its core beliefs about resurrection, eternal life and accompaniment by Jesus. Angus and Josephine both call themselves Christians. Angus was brought up as a Christian, and uses Christian language and structures provided by the church, which help him organise his world. Josephine uses a different Christian language, but the core references are similar. This also helps her organise her world. These structures include a belief in God the Father, Son and Holy Spirit, the belief in Jesus as the Son of God and the belief in the promises of forgiveness, penitence, salvation, return and eternal life. The journey of life is but a herald of the next journey after death, where death has no dominion and where we, in some way, reunite and reconcile ourselves to the infinite God.

As an allegory, the Christian journey is no better expressed than in John Bunyan's *Pilgrim's Progress*. The hero, Christian by name, embarks on a long, compelling and unavoidable journey towards the celestial city in which God resides, which brings him joy, pain and discomfort. He embarks on his journey somewhat reluctantly, but feeling uneasy and dissatisfied with his life. He leaves his wife and children in order to do this, although they catch up with him later. This idea of the suffering journey towards salvation is part of our Christian understanding. The journey of Jesus into his own short life was accompanied by intense suffering but also by great love. Jesus' insistence on love as the method of living is startling and very difficult. But this is what we aspire to, and this gives us our basic value for the care of other people, including older people.

There will be suffering. W.B. Yeats wrote of the despair that accompanies some periods of life in 'The Second Coming', when the 'falcon cannot hear the falconer... when things fall apart'.[41] It is the soul's search, the research and the vigilance that make up the spiritual journey, and at the end of the suffering, we believe, there will be joy and understanding. T.S. Eliot, that great Christian poet, writes of this in *Four Quartets*, as we have already noted. As he is contemplating his own old age and failings, he writes of the journey of exploration that leads us back to the start to see things afresh. The spiritual journey can be accompanied; it is sometimes led by a church life but can be conducted without a church life. A Christian spiritual journey, as we see in Chapter 5, is not necessarily hooked to Christian church life, even among Christians.

Linking the spiritual journey with successful ageing

Negotiation of self in society is part of the spiritual journey. It is in this negotiation that meaning and purpose can be found. It is in the daily detail of life, played out as a relationship between individuals, that the spiritual journey takes form. Our responsibility as spiritual beings is to support each other on our journeys into self.

We have made the case for placing the spiritual journey centrally, as the key mechanism by which we become fully human and retain our shared humanity. Wondering what life is all about is a shared and universal characteristic of all people. The way we wonder and the way we react will differ enormously but the 'wondering' remains, bidden or unbidden, rejected or welcomed. The dark times of our lives make us pause for thought, as do the joyful times. We have suggested that this journey is variously recognised and managed, sometimes in great depth and other times with dismissive contempt. The journey nevertheless continues, despite our attempts to avoid or deny it. The questions of meaning and purpose do not go away, although they may hide beneath the surface. Big life events, like the birth of children, death of parents, start of our working life, end of our school life and childhood, retirement, ill health and our own death prompt uncomfortable thoughts and pause for reflection. As we age, they perhaps become more pressing. This is the basis upon which we conduct our lives, and these are the stories we tell.

The importance and centrality of the spiritual journey must be recognised in the pursuit of 'successful ageing' at both an empirical and a theoretical level.

Revisiting independence

There seems, within this, to be a need to revisit the notion of dependence and independence. The idea of independence is one of the holy grails of the late 20th and early 21st centuries, and is linked to our modern attraction to individualism. This is what we are encouraged to aspire to, in all our life stages. However, in spiritual terms, independence is not the method or the goal. If we take seriously the spiritual journey as our primary task, then we embark on a journey of *interdependence and co-dependence* with our fellow travellers. If we can regain a more *interdependent* definition of independence, we can start to develop a policy and practice of mutual care and can release the potential of older people *to support and comfort* others as well as meet their own needs for support and comfort. The relationship between spiritual carer and cared-for is two-way. *We each care for each other.*

We must try to move to being *alongside* and being in relationship with people rather than meeting targets and achieving goals. Focusing on process rather than outcome is part of the spiritual journey. This is a method of health and social care practice which has extraordinary power, but is surprisingly absent from educational and training programmes in health and social care.

Summary

If we are to take seriously the spiritual care of older people, we must take seriously the idea of the essential and inevitable spiritual journey, which influences and articulates our own ageing and experience of old age. The spiritual carer is someone who can accompany the older person on their spiritual journey, able to hear the spiritual stories and to share their own. The way this is done depends very much on the relationship between the carer and the older person and on the capacities and gifts of both involved. Spiritual accompaniment is about developing an encouraging relationship, one with the other. The ageing and older person may well have concerns, perhaps over legacy and succession, and perhaps about the wider purpose and meaning of their long life, as they look back wistfully and forwards anxiously into an uncertain future. The specifically Christian spiritual relationship tries to use what we believe from the scriptures and from the teachings handed down through Jesus to encourage a positive and optimistic view of the future on a different shore and in a different place. The ideas of coming home, of the rocky road and of return are all deeply embedded in our human psyche. This can be hugely challenging in the face of the vicissitudes of old age, and the diminishments that often come with old age.

Successful ageing theories, as we saw in Chapter 3, suggest that finding balance between competing emotions and actions, between the internal and external world, is the way to achieve contentment in old age. This is variously called individuation, reconciliation, adaptation or coherence. Acknowledging the spiritual journey, whatever its orientation, whichever faith or non-faith it uses as its guide and however mixed and varied these guides are, is *the* primary task for the carer. This means that diminishment must be acknowledged as part of the journey alongside daily achievement and triumphs, however small and mundane. We can learn from the ideas of creative diminishment and creative suffering expressed by Teilhard de Chardin[42] and Paul Tournier,[43] who suggest in different ways that it is *in* the reductions and changes in our old age that we can be our most creative. The spiritual journey into old age is not solely about looking back at the past, but about looking forwards to the future and its possibilities. The triumphs of getting up in the morning and making it to breakfast, writing a letter, reading a book, going out of the house, should not be underestimated. The achievement of decent, honourable and faithful daily living is to be celebrated by carer and cared-for alike. We are all ageing: we are all the same in that respect.

Chapter 5

Attitudes to ageing: implications for spiritual care and support

On a societal level... we tend to fear aging, mistrust it and think of aging as a 'thief in the night'. Our culture has yet to discover the growth, purpose and meaning in aging. We seem to carry around some strange, irrational notion that aging should be avoided, resisted, or pushed away... At all costs, don't let aging happen to you! Because we suffer this age prejudice, we may do an unfortunate thing; we may unconsciously run from our own aging and in so doing deny ourselves the rich, living water that God offers us in maturation.[44]

Old age, of all realities, is perhaps the one of which we retain a purely abstract notion for the longest time.[45]

Introduction

In the previous chapter, we presented an upbeat, hopeful account of the way in which the spiritual journey upon which we all embark can provide opportunities to see ageing as giving scope for spiritual development and maturity. However, we know that most people are fearful of ageing and we have discussed the tendency for people to deny or not recognise their own ageing, and to disassociate themselves from the ageing process: 'I am not ageing, but *you* are ageing.' We have already referred to the parallels in Melanie Klein's idea of childhood development as the growing person moves from what she calls the 'paranoid schizoid' position to the depressive position. In this process, the person begins to accept the other and the self as being in relationship with each other and to some extent accepts the other as a shaping force. People thus learn about their mutuality and individuality. They start to recognise each other more accurately.

In the same way, in old age the 'depressive position' is one in which we start to recognise ourselves as ageing and the ageing of others. We place ourselves in a position of exchange with others, and manage our own ageing within that exchange. We age and perceive ageing in a particular way because of the influences and relationships around us. This is quite a hard thing to do and requires a conscious will to do it.

In this chapter, we think about why we might all be so fearful of and resistant to ageing and how this impacts on our behaviour towards each other. Further, we consider how these attitudes pervade not only our individual and family lives but also our social structures and institutions, and how this in turn can create problems for ageing that are both unnecessary and harmful.

We consider the late work of some notable artists and scholars, where their own experience of ageing promotes the idea that ageing is another 'place', another time, a different season, a 'place' where things must be done differently, and where it might be a joy to do things differently. We propose a way of thinking about ageing and 'doing ageing' which moves us on from fear, resistance and denial to consent and tolerance of the ambivalence of old age, and to the freedoms that consent to ageing and acceptance of ambivalence offer. We think about the implications for spiritual care of these ideas and practices, particularly within a Christian context.

Our general attitudes to ageing

To state the obvious, we live in a cultural situation in the West which is one of rapid change. Old familiar ways of being and doing are being transformed. The *pace* of change in our key activities of daily living is sometimes overwhelming. The accompanying change in our social manners and expectations about our social relationships is startling. It seems things really were different in the old country. This doesn't mean they were better or worse; it is a brave person who would venture an opinion about that, but they were certainly different. Our access to 'cheap' knowledge, opinions, 'likes', and 'friends' has echoes with the ideas of cheap grace proposed by Bonhoeffer.[46] The word 'cheap' means easily come by, 'the grace we bestow upon ourselves'. In these times of internet and speed, we can pick and choose endless 'knowledge' without it having much impact on ourselves or our actions. Every generation, of course, thinks the younger generation is in some way feckless, less respectful of tradition, and the old joke about fusty old people always harking back to the past has an uncomfortable familiarity to it for those who are ageing. We really do start talking like our parents. We really do feel confused about current behaviour and values. We *are* in the past. We, the ageing, are not located in the future. This is a place we cannot go. Keeping up is hard for us all. We are inevitably going to find that the definitions and experience of ageing require change in us.

However, ageing might best be seen as a fluid cluster of ideas and practices, particularly as we find that we can increasingly postpone the ageing of our bodies through medical innovation and technological creativity. In a society where feeling old and experiencing ageing bodies is increasingly negotiable, we have the increasing capacity to redesign ageing, and rethink what ageing might be.

The challenge to the Judeo-Christian vision of ageing

These new ways of approaching ageing challenge the Judeo-Christian tradition in which we are steeped in the West. This tradition offers us a standard picture of life's journey and our ageing trajectory. This had its roots in the medieval understanding of life's journey and was then embellished in later times, as we saw earlier.

Crabbed old age and youth

Paul exhorts his readers not to dishearten their sons and daughters: 'Parents, do not irritate your children, or they will become discouraged' (Colossians 3:21) and Peter in Acts quotes the prophet Joel, who referred to old men having dreams. It seems that old and young have different roles to play, envisioning a future and using dreams to offer some wisdom about the past to inform the future. While the young have their visions and look forward, the aged are dreaming, remembering and looking backwards. Both these activities are important for the stability of society and the acquisition of wisdom, but there are inevitable tensions between the two activities, especially as the whole concept of being old is changing and being challenged. As Pat Thane points out in the last chapter of her wonderful book on the history of old age, these long-received ideas of old age have changed throughout history, and the increasing numbers of older people force a changed understanding of old age. New stereotypes emerge. This time, they offer more hopeful options for older people. Thane writes, 'Only with the late 20th century has old age come to be seen as a stage in life that (with luck, health and freedom) can be enjoyed on its own terms.'[47] This, of course, brings with it other difficulties. The expectations of older people to be more active, to work more years, to be economically useful, hands-on grandparents, to look young and vigorous, to remain fully engaged in the structures of midlife and so on, mean that those who can't or won't do these things and who more easily fit in to the old stereotypes are at a disadvantage. Either way, it's a bit of a battle.

Our actual ageing experience and possibilities depend on our external circumstances, our relationships with others and our own received stereotypes of ageing. We live up to the expectations of those around us: to paraphrase Richard Bach, 'Argue for your limitations and they will be yours.' In this context, let us think about how Angus and Josephine have experienced their ageing.

ANGUS' ageing

Angus had spent most of his life happily avoiding any discussion of, or thinking seriously about, his old age. It was only when his beloved, his confiding 'other', became ill and was clearly going to die that he started to feel old. He began to complain about aches and pains, greatly increased his visits to the GP and referred to himself as an 'old man'. This was partly because he was seeing his wife deteriorate and become old and ill. He found himself to be mirrored in her illness. He started to sleep less well, found himself getting up in the night, got backache and found that his appetite changed. He started to creak and groan. He no longer enjoyed food and drink in the way he had done in the past. He couldn't taste the food so well. All these changes took place during his beloved's demise and death. He felt like an old man as he buried her, and allowed himself to be nurtured and fussed over by his children during this time. He seemed unable to make clear decisions, he lost his enthusiasm for driving and his confidence in his abilities to do simple things. He lost some weight and felt weaker generally. It was hard to say whether his behaviour and symptoms were a consequence of ageing, or a consequence of bereavement and fear. Very typically, of course, both these phenomena in our lives happen at the same time. We grow older, a 'beloved' dies and we are plunged into a state of grief. This is a pattern. Our feelings of being old are often prompted by grief and the loss of a beloved.

Angus didn't have a strong sense of self separate from his beloved. His ageing task after his wife's death was to find himself again. He located his despair at the time of her death in his body and in what he called his old age – by this time he was 80. In truth, Angus was very well, cognitively sharp, strong and capable. In practice, he took on the mantle of old age almost as a protection. He accepted, indeed almost welcomed, the stereotypes. And these stereotypes were convenient and useful for his children as well. In their new-found role of 'carer for father', they confirmed certain expectations with which he would now conform. He would visit them and be 'looked after'. They would phone regularly, visit and fuss around his kitchen, tutting about the lack of edible food and 'sell-by' dates. They would insist that he phoned them if he went out in the car. Between them and with the collusion of Angus, they created a mutually reassuring dependency. He was the old childlike father; they were the responsible younger grown-ups. This suited them all. Later, we will see how he threw this image off again as he progressed through his 80s.

JOSEPHINE's ageing

Josephine's trajectory into old age was different. Josephine, as we have seen, was far from physically able. Her 'descent' into old age, or the perception that she was now old, started with one incident: the fall on the church steps and the fractured femur. In that moment, she moved from competent, useful, charming Josephine, to worrisome, frail, 'needing care', old Josephine. She managed to get out of hospital following this fall owing to strong wishes, articulate requests, loving friends and neighbours and a local district nurse team who supported her. The fact that she had loving friends and neighbours and a willing healthcare team was, in part, testament to her character and deeds over many years. However, following the fall, she was struggling to move around her house even with a Zimmer. She was becoming incontinent. She had a variety of 'carers', paid and unpaid, who visited and tutted and made noises about residential care, and about safety and security. Josephine, aged 90, had no illusions about the struggle ahead in terms of her deteriorating body, but she also knew that the main struggle was to maintain herself *and others' perception of herself* as a fully functioning adult in the face of such deterioration. When a nurse is wiping your bottom like a baby, it is hard to feel like a competent adult, even with the most sensitive of care. Standing up to social stereotypes and 'oughts' and 'shoulds' is very challenging at the best of times. When you are feeling unwell, it is twice as difficult.

Josephine did not fear age; she feared the imposition of stereotypes that came with deteriorating health: the assumption, for instance, that being forgetful about names of visitors was a sign of creeping dementia. The 'caring' visitors eagerly looked for signs of deterioration to build their case for residential care. They hardly knew they were doing this, of course. They, in turn, were responding to the received ideas of frailty and ageing trajectories. The effort to maintain herself in the face of such stereotyping was exhausting, and being exhausted compromises the resolve to fight for oneself. The fight may become belligerent, passively aggressive, uncooperative and unpleasant to the carer. This did not happen in Josephine's case because of her grace. She was able to interpret her own furies and fears within her faith and via her spiritual life and practices, and in this way settle herself. This grace was transmitted to her carers, who treated her with great respect and contained their worry. She was 'at risk', however, and the institutional machinery of health and social care organisations doesn't like taking risks, for understandable reasons including exposure to litigation or complaint. Where there is risk, there is blame, responsibility and danger. She was under daily pressure to conform to the stereotypes of 'at risk and needing residential care'. How long she could continue her resistance, and with what methods, we shall see later.

Both Angus and Josephine have found themselves in different ways manoeuvred into old age by their circumstances. It is not the chronological age itself that determines old age, but also the circumstances that surround the ageing person. It is, as we have seen with both Angus and Josephine, to some extent a question of what others can tolerate. Living with the ambivalence and uncertainty of old age is a challenge for us all. Carers of those who are ageing have a responsibility to think about these things for themselves and for those for whom they care.

The ambivalence towards old age

The ambivalence towards old age that we all feel is well expressed by the two quotes at the start of this chapter. Marcel Proust was particularly horrified by the ageing body. He describes going to a ball, where he sees grotesque figures dancing and greeting him and is confused by who these people are. His description reminds one of a Bruegel painting. Ugly, grimacing figures leer at him. He is frightened. Then he realises that these faces are the faces of his friends and, worse still, his face is also cast in the same manner.

The ambivalence towards 'future old age' is very apparent, and commented upon by Kathleen Woodward in her very interesting book on the discontents of old age.[48] She considers works of literature in which ageing is discussed, in order to try and understand how ageing is perceived. She criticises Freud's stark fear of ageing, and his view that youth and age are the greatest opposites of which human life is capable. She suggests that, as a society, we are profoundly ambivalent about old age, and mostly negative about it. When she discusses Proust's work, she demonstrates a deep ambivalence on the part of Marcel to the future. This seems to be the crux of the problem: the timeless future, full of hope, perceived by youth, and the contrasting hopeless future with limited time perceived by the ageing. These seem incompatible. Later, we will think about the intergenerational relationships fundamental to the caring relationship, and how these have an impact on understandings of age and care.

The tipping points

What we can see from our growing understanding of Angus and Josephine is that there are tipping points, crossroad moments, when specific ageing paths are taken. The most important obvious tipping point is a medical drama that changes the relationship of the person to their world; this might be, as we have seen with Josephine, a fall. There is a very typical trajectory after a fall in old age: the fallen person needs hospitalising to attend to a broken bone and, in the process, loses some of their mobility and their daily living skills. Activities of daily living are measured and found to be wanting. The person seems confused, is declared to be frail and is put into a category that highlights the need for extra care, either at home or sometimes in residential care. The service response to the medical drama varies from place to place, and we know from recent press coverage that it ranges from very poor to excellent. The upshot is the creation of a publicly acknowledged frail older person who needs support in one way or the other. The assumption that there will be family support underpins future discussions. The community care push of the 1980s and the subsequent legislation of the 1990s implicitly assumed care by family as it struggled to move the focus of care from hospital to community. (We discuss this in more detail in Chapter 6.)

Sometimes the medical situation is not an emergency, but creeps up and *becomes* an emergency. For instance, an elderly couple, David and Cath, married for many years and living in the country, have one or two rather scary encounters in their car with other drivers while David is driving. Consequently, they decide that they will only drive to the local shops. This limits their social life, which used to involve visiting friends further afield and meeting for lunch on occasions in the local town. Now they have reduced their social environment. The husband, David, always a fine walker, wanders further afield, and finds himself in unknown territory. His wife, Cath, is alarmed when he is brought home in a confused state by a passing driver, who has seen him on the road. The driver, who knows David, says that David didn't seem to know where he lived. They further restrict their movements to only walking very locally. Lack of social stimulation and fear of the consequences of overexposure mean that their lives reduce in their capacity. They watch TV more. David sleeps much more. His wife notices small changes in his mood and capacities. David then gets a urine infection, which sends him into a delirious state. The doctor is called, David is medicated, he reacts badly to the medication and eventually he is admitted to hospital with a raging infection and a high temperature. Cath no longer drives at all, and so she needs help to visit him.

People rally around and their daughter, who lives many miles away, starts to actively help. This puts a strain on the daughter's life. David doesn't seem to be recovering, and although he has no temperature his behaviour is odd in the ward, sitting with the nurses, laughing inappropriately, wandering around. His behaviour seems unpredictable. The acute ward into which he was admitted is not equipped to cope with this kind of behaviour. They want him out; they need the beds. A period of respite in a home is suggested, and, after some weeks in hospital, a bed in the local residential home is found for a two-week period. David is restless in the home: Cath feels guilty and distressed. Their daughter goes home back to her own life and work, leaving Cath to visit when she can. It becomes clear that David cannot go home. He has stopped eating, and wanders aimlessly. When Cath is asked to fill out a form for the home to tell them something about her husband, she realises that, on reflection, his daily living habits have been a bit odd for a while. It is only when she pauses to think about it that she realises he has been wandering for months, he has been eating badly for months and he has been sleeping erratically. He is admitted permanently into a residential care setting and never goes home. Everybody is upset.

These two situations of medical drama or creeping frailty are very common indeed. The precarious balance required to manage ageing is upset in both cases. In both cases, the person involved becomes categorised as old as they succumb to the frailties of their bodies. We become old as our bodies start to fail us: bodily changes show us that ageing is taking place. We get grey hairs, we start showing wrinkles, we sag, we ache and so on. However, all these can be tolerated until there is a crisis or situation that requires us to change our practices. Then we take a further step into old age.

We have seen in Chapter 2 that there is much thinking around stages of life. Many writers have conceptualised ageing as a staged process, like the seasons. We start to notice our age at the end of the summer: we wilt a bit, things change, we start to feel different, but it's all very subtle stuff. Then, just as the leaves change colour and finally fall, we also start to change colour. Our hue changes, we begin to look different and to look differently on the world. As we approach our winter, the colours can be glorious, but there is also a sense of time passing and of knowing that the next spring will not be our spring. This idea of stages of old age is used in health and social care practice and research, to distinguish 'young–old' and 'old–old'. Typically, the 'old–old' are counted from the age of 80.

One of the main markers of becoming old is when we stop being economically productive. We discuss this in greater detail in Chapter 9.

Why are we fearful of ageing?

One of the key questions that we must tackle, if we are to think in any useful way about ageing, is why we are fearful of it. The obvious and most simple answer to this question is that ageing is followed by death, and we are fearful of death. However, it seems to be rather more complicated than that. Getting to the bottom of individual fears of ageing provides us with the clues to what spiritual care and support might look like and be required by individuals as they work out their own salvation as they age. If, for instance, a person is very confident of a future life beyond this earthly life in a heavenly setting with past remembrances and relationships reconciled, then *in theory* fear of death will be less about what happens afterwards, and may focus on pain and distress during the process of dying. If another person is very concerned about past sins, and conceptualises the afterlife as a series of stages of purgatory where sins are expunged, then their fears may well be about the degree to which the expunging will be difficult and painful. Knowing what frightens the person is the key, but of course they may well not know themselves. Knowing our fears and anxieties and looking at them boldly is the core of our spiritual journey, and the purpose of spiritual care and support.

What this means is that our ageing makes us aware, willing or not, that our time on earth is short, and that it becomes harder and harder to see *ourselves* as the central purpose of our life. As we grow up and older, we try to develop away from an entirely self-centred view of the world into rounded human beings who understand how other people might think and feel about the world, and about relationships within it. The psychological development required means that, ideally, we go on learning, albeit slowly and painfully, that we are one of many. The universality of ageing is a further reminder that we are not unique individuals, and that our stay on earth is but a short sojourn. The words of the Venerable Bede seem to express this perfectly:

> It seems to me that the life of man on earth is like the swift flight of a single sparrow through the banqueting hall where you are sitting at dinner on a winter's day with your captains and counsellors. In the midst, there is a comforting fire to warm the hall. Outside, the storms of winter rain and snow are raging. This sparrow flies swiftly in through one window of the hall and out through another. While he is inside, the bird is safe from the winter storms, but after a few moments of comfort, he vanishes from sight into the wintry world from which he came. So, man appears on earth for a little while – but of what went before this life, or what follows, we know nothing.[49]

Although we matter deeply to a few, our specific life experience is irrelevant to most others. We must learn to love ourselves as we love others, and we must learn to love God. Loving God moves us away from our self-centre, and puts us in a much wider context. As the baby fears that mother is gone for ever if she leaves the room, so perhaps the ageing woman fears that she is gone for ever if she leaves the world. It is maybe this fear of irrelevance and pointlessness that drives us to create beautiful things, to write profound thoughts, to procreate, to be of service to others. It may also drive some of us to try to destroy each other in order that we can retain the illusion of our centrality. Unless we can get to grips with our fears of irrelevance and pointlessness, we will find our own ageing traumatic. The spiritual journey is a journey of knowing oneself and then applying that knowledge to whatever situation prevails.

So, we would argue that our fear of ageing stems from the fear of irrelevance and annihilation. This is often expressed as a fear of loss of control. In our study on expert elders, the respondents were asked about their current fears. These turned out to concern their possibility of loss of independence or 'edge'. More specifically, these were fears about giving up what they saw as productive work, and somehow losing their main purpose and meaning, fears about mental health problems, particularly depression and dementia, fears about having to move into residential or nursing home care which would mean they were treated like sheep, fears of falling because of the ensuing sequence of events, and fears of being a burden. These fears had caused them to start to change their behaviour, and limit their horizons. The *fear* of ageing, not ageing itself, renders people less free to be who they are, and to age as themselves.

It is fair to say that most research tells us that the fear of ageing is much stronger in those who are still grappling with their middle age. Those who have reached an understanding about old age and about their own ageing and who accept themselves as 'old' are much less fearful. We know that some economic studies have shown that declarations of satisfaction and happiness with life increase as people age despite, it seems, an increase in disability and loss.[50] Happiness, measured in 72 different countries, started high in youth, dipped in midlife and rose again in older age. This seemed to be the case irrespective of social and economic circumstances. However, other studies have shown that it is only in the rich, Western, English-speaking countries that happiness and life satisfaction increase in this way. One explanation for the possibility that happiness increases as we age is that we can shed some of the responsibilities and worries of midlife and that we can become ourselves at last. This is a very popular theme in literature, and it seems that it may have some basis in our social experiences. This was the case with the over-80s in our expert elders study. They did not fear ageing, but they feared the loss of independence and ability to assert themselves. They were making efforts to downsize and to selectively disengage, so that things could remain the same for them.

As Christians, we are encouraged to lose ourselves in Christ, and in so doing to become free. This freedom is about freedom from sin that holds us in the earthly world. This idea of movement away from earthly ties is explored by many writers. This is a place where different values and concerns dominate the daily landscape. This reinforces the idea of journey into old age.

'No country for old men'

When W.B. Yeats wrote 'Sailing to Byzantium', he described it as a metaphor for the spiritual journey into old age. He saw Byzantium as the destination, and as a metaphor for enlightenment and God. The world, with all its demands and youthful pulls, is one from which the aged must pull away to sustain and find themselves, and to avoid being stereotyped. This is a journey of reconciliation and humility.

An aged man is but a paltry thing,
A tattered coat upon a stick, unless
Soul clap its hands and sing, and louder sing
For every tatter in its mortal dress,
Nor is there singing school but studying
Monuments of its own magnificence;
And therefore, I have sailed the seas and come
To the holy city of Byzantium.[51]

Here, Yeats, using his own experience of ageing having reached 60, seems to suggest that age can be stereotyped and diminished, unless 'soul clap its hands and sing'. The journey encourages the singing.

This implies a deeper understanding; a need for reflection and reinterpretation. This is quite like James Hillman's description of 'improving one's biography'.[52] We shall discuss this task of life review in more detail in Chapter 8.

Similarly, the poet Czesław Miłosz, who won the Nobel Prize in Literature in 1980, wrote about the journey into old age as being a journey into a different 'province of life', a new place. This idea of old age being a specifically different setting, and a place where things can be seen and experienced differently, is a dominant and important theme.

There is a conventional notion that ageing confers a spirit of reconciliation and serenity on late works of art, often expressed as some kind of transformation of reality. But age and ill health might produce not serenity but intransigence: what if age and ill health don't produce serenity? There is a danger of being too romantic about old age. We have to be brave to face old age well. The journey is tough.

The implications of these attitudes to ageing: denial or consent

It seems that we have choices as to how we approach and 'do' our ageing. There is the choice about where we understand God to be, in relation to ourselves. Much spiritual care depends on the conceptualisation of God held by individuals as they age. Our attitude to God influences our attitude to old age. Our socio-economic and cultural milieux, and the psychological consequences and influences upon those, give us our positioning of God. God might reside within us, and be an immanent presence, or God might reside externally as a presence 'out there'. Neville Symington expresses this most clearly.[53] He talks from his own painful experience about his perceptions of the angry, punitive God, who he describes as initially external to him, making judgements and meting out punishments. Later in his life, he can see God as internal, within himself, and as a loving God who wants the best for him. But it takes a long time, his lifetime, for him to work through these changes. Gerard Hughes, too, provides us with very rich and stimulating thought about the immanence of God, as well as the transcendence.[54] However, most of us don't investigate these relationships so thoroughly. If we are to understand our spiritual needs and those of others, an understanding of where God is for us is important. This suggests that a spiritual friend or carer should look for this in some way or another.

Having established the presence of God and the assumed nature of God, there is a further choice to be made regarding ageing. There is the journey of denial, which means that we tend to be anti-ageing, that we refuse to accept the process of ageing; we become self-absorbed, maintaining our narcissistic stance, and this can lead to stagnation. We insist on remaining in the 'first half' (we discuss the idea of first and second half of life in Chapter 8). We will not change, and then we find we *cannot* change; ultimately and ironically, we *lose* control by trying to retain it.

The alternative is to *consent* to ageing: to allow ourselves to become older, to enter this new place, and in so doing to let in some light and some possibilities of change. This is arguably a journey into the real self, and a chance for integration and reconciliation. This consent becomes easier if we understand the context in which we age. This is where we now focus our attention.

Chapter 6

The context in which we age

Show a people as one thing, as only one thing, over and over again, and that is what they become... the single story robs people of dignity.[55]

This chapter continues the discussion about our ageing journey and the spiritual imperative by looking in some detail at the context in which we currently negotiate our ageing.

The pressures of contemporary life

At a recent church wedding we attended, the minister gave an address to the young couple. He pointed up three serious challenges to a happy and sustaining marriage.

Firstly, the fact that the young couple may well live a long way away from their base community and parents, so community support becomes more difficult. There is a geographical and time hurdle. Secondly, the rise in self-centredness among people generally. We have referred to this in Chapter 5, regarding the idea of narcissism. As we mature, we hope to shed this narcissistic dominance, but this becomes more difficult in a world where the self is the *subject* of knowledge, rather than the purveyor and absorber of knowledge. The immediate and pressing concerns of activities of daily living are challenge enough. We all have different daily struggles just to get through the day: 'How will I get to work on time, when will I do the washing, who is using the car today, is there anything in the fridge that we can eat?' These take precedence over selfless caring and thought for others. Thirdly, time is becoming a commodity. Most people have very limited time to rest and pause and think. Families and individuals are hostage to a mentality of 24-hours-a-day, seven-days-a-week alertness, either through their internet connections or in terms of expectation and availability of most services. Time pressures, and the perception that time runs away with us, is something to which we have already alluded in Chapter 2. The precious commodity of time is in short supply for all as we create more rules and goals and targets for ourselves.

These three challenges to a young married couple apply equally to the ageing person and give pause for thought (although, happily, the young couple went ahead regardless!).

The context is always changing from generation to generation, of course, as we have discussed in Chapter 5. Our mothers, born in the 1920s, were expected to marry and not to enter the working environment after their marriage. World War II deeply influenced their life's trajectories. Our grandparents' ageing a generation earlier was mediated and influenced by an assumption of decline and forgetfulness in old age, and by a general societal tolerance, a benignly patronising approach to the elderly, and by strong village-community lives which, surrounded them if not with love, then certainly with an unspoken expectation of 'knowing one's place' and of duty to be done.

Being aware of the key influences on a particular individual, as well as the wider environment in which they negotiate ageing, helps us to understand their spiritual life and needs. Each person has a unique context in which they age, but each generation shares some influences that shape attitudes to ageing.

Let us return to Angus and Josephine.

ANGUS' context

Angus has two middle-aged children, who have young children of their own and busy lives, living hundreds of miles away in both cases. The family relationships are warm and concerned, and there is a general sense of goodwill that flows between the generations. In Angus' case, family is a good and positive influence. However, both his children need to find a way of managing to continue to be warm and loving with their ageing dad, now that their mother, who played that central coordinating role, has died. Family and responsibilities towards family suddenly become more complicated. Who will visit and how often? How will they negotiate Angus' old-age needs between them? What language can they use? What happens if Angus needs care? They are all propelled out of their comfortable and stable mutual support, into something different. Family relationships have changed. Tensions arise; schedules are compared, pecking orders and old wounds resurface.

Friendships that Angus has with contemporaries seem less complicated somehow. These remain relatively stable after his wife's death. Common experiences, in this case widowhood, confirm and reinforce friendships. Angus' established long-term friendships, developed over many years of living in the same place, confirm his continued value as lunch guest, golf partner and raconteur. Indeed, his social value, as a single male, increases.

Angus' friends form part of his key community, which includes church attendance and activities. This community remains stable. His ageing is protected by this community, and by his general economic and political security. So, superficially as we have seen, his ageing is managed, moderate and mild. The family look to this community to continue the long-established relationships, and new visiting patterns are established which are acceptable and eagerly anticipated by all concerned.

Two years later, Angus remarries, and this throws all the social stability into turmoil, but it cements the understanding that Angus is now no longer in need of 'care'. The responsibility shifts to his new wife. Angus' ageing trajectory is completely disrupted – an upsurge of love, the demands and attentions of a new wife, have provided Angus with the impetus he needs to reject the ageing, declining stereotype. He feels well, he looks well and as he ploughs on he leaves in his wake confused, hurt and 'put out' family and community friends, who had him pigeonholed into a comfortable, predictable decline. His 'cloud of glory' casts a shadow on others. He is not 'doing' ageing as expected. He is disrupting the pattern.

JOSEPHINE's context

Josephine has a different context. She has no immediate family and has never been married. She has a loving cousin's daughter who keeps in touch, but that kinship relation is not expected socially to take any kind of responsibility for her. Josephine's frailty, and lack of obvious family carer, mean that she becomes a public health and social care 'problem'. Her ageing is a matter of public visibility. Her local community (as with Angus) is very supportive, but in her case is also very anxious, both about Josephine's prospects and about the impact of her ageing trajectory. Her incontinence, the state of her small house and her declining abilities are the subject of discussion outside her home. Angus' occasional toileting mishap or cognitive error has remained a private matter between him and his new wife: Josephine's ageing is directly affected by the funding policies of health and social care, and the possibility of support to meet her wishes to stay at home. She wants to remain at home. Her choices are limited. She is influenced by her antipathy to residential care. She has an image of residential care that is rooted in an understanding of the 'poor house' and the stereotypes associated with that. Despite her common sense and knowledge that things have moved on, she still retains the stereotype. Josephine knows that her chances of retaining her 'Josephine-ness' in the face of her limited choices are slim. However, she can draw on her inner faith and find some meaning and solace in graceful diminishment, or 'creative diminishment'.

Both Angus and Josephine conduct their ageing in a context of policy and practice set by different influencing institutions. We will now look at these in a bit more detail, considering some of the paradoxes inherent within them.

Some contextual complexities

As we have seen in Chapter 2, family experiences profoundly influence our development. There are two aspects to this in relation to ageing. Firstly, our early childhood attachments will influence the way we age, and, secondly, our immediate family circumstances as we age are significant in the process.

The link between early childhood and later life

It is well known that our earliest experiences of attachment as babies will affect our lifelong development, and that these experiences shape our character and personality. Poor attachment brings with it difficulties in forming mature relationships, and in taking responsibility for our negative difficult emotions. Individuals deal uniquely with poor attachment. There is no direct line from poor attachment to difficulties in navigating ageing, but there is a link between immaturity and movement through life's stages. Poor attachment at an early stage means that we are more likely to remain in a narcissistic comfort zone, nervous about making generous commitments to parts of life we cannot control and which therefore fill us with terror. Our early life experiences form and shape us, and we spend our lives winnowing, refining and sometimes transforming ourselves in response to these. If we have a contented and secure childhood where we feel loved, we are more likely to form our own contented and secure family in turn, who are more likely to respond to our ageing frailties with love and concern. James Hillman writes about the formation of character, and suggests that it is character that determines the ageing experience.[56] While this feels uncomfortable in some respects, because life experiences are often thrust on to people who have no control over them, nevertheless the development of character through the influences of family, education, community and spiritual life has consequences for ageing. People rarely change much without specific attempts to do so.

Care: family or public?

One of the paradoxes of our current social situation in the UK is that we have health and social care systems based on policies that firmly state that people should and want to remain in their own homes and with their families. These policies increasingly rely on family support. This is at the same time as our family structures and relationships are undergoing major change, and experiencing great pressure from the current global economic and political situation in which we find ourselves.

Families are no longer predictably structured. Divorce, remarriage, stepfamilies, blended families and civil partnerships mean that the traditional idea that 'the daughter' will be the main carer is shot through with contradictions. The coherent, close, loving family who are geographically present can no longer be the basis of our planning. We must think about family context. Family relationships can be used as methods of retaliation, punishment, sanction, greed, envy and entitlement as much as they can be sources of kindness, support and compassion. This is a hugely complicated area into which a spiritual carer should enter only with great care.

Ageing population and stigma

As we age, we experience the tensions concerning the perception of an ageing population. We become that population, and we learn that our ageing is a 'trouble' to the rest of society. Although the demographics have been known for years, the reality of a shift in population structure has only recently been recognised. 'They' have become 'us'. Nearly a third of the UK population is now over the age of 60; age is no longer a minority status. The patronising indulgence of old age as a relative rarity cannot be sustained with such an increase in numbers.

Older people have purchasing power and political power through the ballot box. The degree to which ageing is now seen as a trouble or a problem is, of course, linked to money. The state has a duty and commitment to care for its older people. The 'cradle-to-grave' assumption is still in place. The more elders there are, the more it costs. The state has limited funds and political imperatives to keep national contribution reasonable. Tax is a sore point for all political parties. The balance between people paying tax to support the state policies, and those receiving the benefit of the state policies, is changing. State pensions are funded by the working generation. The solution to the imbalance between the taxpayers and the recipients of state old-age pension benefits is currently to delay the state pension age and to encourage continual working lives and private investments in pensions from an early age. This is in the context of enormous global uncertainty.

In the UK, the over-50s, the baby boomers, are perceived as 'having it best'. Property values, and the encouragement of home ownership in the currently elderly generation, have combined to create a group who are mortgage-free and capital-'rich'. At the same time, the younger generation is struggling to get on to the property ladder. This generation of final-salary pensioners is probably the last of its kind. However, this generation must increasingly pay for their old-age care and they will live much longer and therefore suffer the vicissitudes of old age, disability, loss and co-morbidity for longer periods of time. They too will need care.

However, the paradox remains that the longer we live, itself a cause for celebration, the longer we must look to services to support us, which costs money. Living much longer can be seen as a mark of successful ageing, but brings with it the dysfunctions of old age. The aspiration in the late 20th century was to compress morbidity, through medical technical advance (for example, joint and vascular surgery) so that people could be healthy, active and well right until the end of their lives. This was intended to reduce pressure on health and social care services, and improve quality of life, but of course it also increases that pressure. Longevity, the goal of all, is accompanied by increasing chronic diseases of diabetes, stroke, heart disease, cancer, dementia and depression. The longer you live, the more likely you are to experience one of these unfriendly giants. If you live in relative deprivation, you are even more likely to experience these. Money helps.

There are increasingly complex social and moral issues to address when it comes to providing care and support for older people. Sex life in older people has only recently emerged into polite society as an acceptable topic for discussion, although it has long been an unspoken 'problem' facing staff in care homes, to name but one group. However, as we live longer in an explicitly sexualised culture, we will inevitably experience sexual needs and desires that are as variable as those of the younger generation. While sexual needs and intimacy desires change, we need to remember the plight of people living with dementia and those living in residential care; consent in these circumstances is becoming an issue for discussion and concern, as capacity to make valid decisions is more frequently (and rightly) pondered. How can a good society foster and support older people's sexual enjoyment, arguably a 'right', if family members are to hold reins of responsibility as main carers? What impact will such considerations have on the sex lives of older people in care homes? Can different generations overcome the taboos of discussing sex with each other in order to enable healthy sex lives, helpful as they are to good mental health? Are family members ready for discussion about their widowed and cognitively impaired mother developing an affectionate relationship with a man newly arrived in her care home?

Beyond the writing of wills and powers of attorney, a further increasingly pressing concern is the writing of advanced directives, and the wish increasingly expressed by the ill to determine one's own mode of dying. Euthanasia is an inevitable and hugely important aspect of the discussion about how we wish to age. This is particularly so as we extend our lives into extreme old age and potential disability and frailty. In youth, we often can and do express clearly that we would not want to live a life of extreme disability and decrepitude; this isn't necessarily so in older age and frailty. Things change: can we be certain that our ideas in relative youth are how we will feel at a later stage? What are our review arrangements? Who can make these decisions for us in the event of loss of our own capacity to decide? This is not the subject of this book, but these are nevertheless moral questions about the meaning and purpose of old age and ageing, and refer to the question posed in Chapter 2.

When families are the main source of care and support, with all the implied financial powers, and when societal resources are scarce, then the idea that your increasingly dependent relative might live to 100 might well seem oppressive and diminishing to the hard-pressed 'children'. It might well seem oppressive to the ageing person as well. Deciding to take control of the nature and timing of the end of our life to avoid what we assume will be the distresses and disabilities of extreme old age requires robust moral reasoning, as well as discussions with family and friends and paid care staff. We note without surprise how slow our legislators are to grasp this nettle. Both these enduring psychological issues, sex and death, will become increasingly pertinent to the Christian ageing person and must be part of the discussion of the context in which we age. We might well look to spiritual support in thinking through these matters.

The context of spiritual care

We now know that an active engagement in spiritual life contributes to well-being and health.[57] We have discussed this in Chapter 4. Harold Koenig has been prolific in producing research that investigates the relationship between religion and ageing, which shows largely positive associations between the two.[58] However, in the current context of multifaith societies and sensitivities about the dominance of any one faith, the linking of spirituality with any faith, or with the idea of a transcendent or immanent being, is greeted with some alarm in the public sector. So, while *spiritual* care is increasingly understood to be a good thing within a caring service or environment, an explicitly religious focus is not. This makes Christian spiritual care-giving complex. The development of healthcare chaplaincy is a good example of these tensions.[59]

The rise in spiritual interest and the decline of religious adherence

We find ourselves in a situation of tension and paradox in our understanding of spirituality. There is an acknowledged decrease generally in religiosity in the UK. There is a decline in church attendance.[60] The populations of church are ageing. There is a crisis in clerical recruitment. People are leaving the church, despite still retaining their faith. There is at the same time a similar tension and attempt at redefinition within health and social care services, where manageable definitions are sought of what it means to provide a meaningful health and social care service to individuals, where demand always outstrips supply. There are interesting parallels in the way that both these institutions (church and health) are required to reconstruct themselves to meet expressed need. In the health service, collaboration is promoted between public and private, health and social care, volunteers and families on the basic assumption that collaboration produces more coherent care for those who need it. In the church, there is a similar difficulty in finding a methodology that can support the intuitive belief that active interest in spirituality and religion is linked to well-being and health. Things are changing, and they need to change for the core beliefs in the power of the spirit to remain the same, and be liberated as a health and well-being resource.

The decline in Christian church attendance and religiosity has caught the attention of academics in several different disciplines. This is partly because other changes are taking place that are related to the *increase* in interest in spiritual matters. While the religiosity of the population is declining, interest in spirituality is increasing. People are increasingly looking for purpose and meaning outside religious traditions. While our churches are emptying, our need and search for spiritual meaning apparently surges, and becomes more explicit and socially acceptable, as for example David Hay[61] and more recently Linda Woodhead suggest.[62]

Interest in spiritual issues and the rise of individualism

People are expressing more interest in spiritual matters. The Western 'baby boomers', who are the next generation of older people, have spread the net wide in a search for purpose and meaning. Personal spirituality has become somewhat conflated with a rise in the supremacy of the individual. There seems to be confusion between the assertion of the *rights* of the individual in society, and the search for self in relationship with a higher being. Individualism, which began its modern journey with the Renaissance, has now become embedded in our everyday understandings and assumptions of what it is to be human. The general principle is that the individual has supremacy over the collective. This means that we take for granted our rights as unique and important individuals to live independent lives. It is the role of our major social institutions to support our individualism, and this is enshrined in 'policy and practice' of needs-led, evidence-based, person-centred models of caring practice. We are living in a world now where individual rights and needs are more and more seen as the central mechanism by which we drive our society. These two phenomena – the rise of the individual as the central focus of policy and the rise of the interest in the spiritual – are often linked together and it is important to unpack that relationship further.

The rise in individualism is linked to political expediency, and to philosophical and economic preference. It has been argued that individualism is yet another turn of the wheel of capitalism, since it encourages extreme narcissism, which is hooked to expenditure and wealth accumulation.

The search for the spirit within oneself is essentially about acceding to the will of God to find oneself, and is a very different process from the pursuit of worldly rights and individual recognition. As we become less interested in community and 'society',[63] and more interested in 'ourselves', so we lose one of our core meanings – that of community building. This prompts a series of existential questions about meaning, place and purpose of self. The 2016 Reith Lectures were on this very subject of identity. The 'Brexit' and the Scottish independence referenda are examples of these questions.

Implications of the current context for spiritual care

The *context* in which we age is a key influence on that ageing; we have seen that Angus and Josephine's immediate and historical influences shaped their approach to, and experience of, ageing. There are some complexities in our social experience of ageing which present us with paradoxes; for instance, an implicit reliance on families to take responsibility for the care of ageing relatives, at a time when family structures are changing considerably. The social policies have not yet caught up with the lived realities of social life. There are currently great uncertainties about the future in our Western world; in the UK and elsewhere, we are trying to make sense of a rise in populism that may have transformative influences on our way of life, and on our ability to plan for our future.

Spiritual support and care, particularly in the Christian tradition, focuses on the importance of allowing God to lead and our being willing to follow, of our being less anxious about our lives and more trusting in God. We are asked to have faith that all will be well:

> This is why I tell you: do not be worried about the food and drink you need in order to stay alive, or about clothes for your body. After all, isn't life worth more than food? And isn't the body worth more than clothes? Look at the birds: they do not sow seeds, gather a harvest and put it in barns; yet your Father in heaven takes care of them! Aren't you worth much more than birds? Can any of you live a bit longer by worrying about it?
> MATTHEW 6:25–27

So the message is, as ever: 'Do not be anxious about your life.' This is a hard message to believe and act upon in our present situation and context, which still seem to offer considerable room for improvement in our health and social care systems and in the ethical thinking underpinning them. We will require spiritual perseverance, particularly in the face of the vicissitudes of old age, to which we now turn.

Chapter 7

The discontents of ageing

Lord, how long will I live?
   When will I die?
   Tell me how soon my life will end.
How short you have made my life!
   In your sight my lifetime seems nothing.
Indeed every living being is no more than a puff of wind,
   no more than a shadow.
All we do is for nothing;
   We gather wealth, but don't know who will get it.
What then can I hope for, Lord?
   I put my hope in you.

PSALM 39:4–7

Introduction

This chapter leads us into the second part of the book, where we consider the possibilities, opportunities and practicalities for growth and change as we age. We started by identifying the pervasive 'us-and-them' language about ageing, and by noting that for us all to age well we must start thinking of ourselves as all in it together: we are all ageing. To help each other age well, we should start young. By creating the division between ageing and not ageing, we do ourselves no service at all. In Chapter 2, we considered the nature of ageing, posing the question, 'What is ageing for?' We asserted the importance of using the inevitable ageing trajectory as an opportunity to grow and to develop spiritually. In the subsequent three chapters, we considered the paradoxical context in which we currently age, and also the links and contrasts between our preconceived and research-based ideas of successful ageing and the spiritual journey. We have thought about the way in which attitudes to age influence our experience of ageing, and where those dominant attitudes have arisen. In this bridging chapter, we face the discontents of old age. By this, we mean the things that make us fearful and nervous about embracing old age as a new, stimulating, often exciting and sometimes very lengthy stage of life; let us then name the possibilities of disability, of mental illness, the certainty of suffering loss, of dying and death, and finally the great temptation of meaninglessness.

Illness, societal management and the need for a common voice

There is currently much hand-wringing, expressed through our media, about the plight of ill older people. Stories abound of people being shunted around hospitals, blocking beds and being unable to return home with support because of lack of local authority funding to provide such support. This seems to be an inevitable component of care, in which many of us participate as volunteers, and its dispiriting effects need to be weighed by us all.

Stories abound, too, of exhausted family members, struggling to cope at home with the demands of a very dependent older relative. This situation is a shared, societal responsibility and, given the complexities of relationships within families or marriages, cannot be ducked by hiding behind platitudes about 'caring communities' or 'a big society'. We need to recognise our own ageing and the realities of an ageing population. We should try to have at least some compassion for our politicians, who often struggle to promote the rational amid societal narcissism: if we are to be serious about our concerns for the care of older people, which will in time inevitably become concerns for the care of ourselves, we will need to support and even encourage those politically unpopular decisions, to increase funding and resources through taxation of some kind.

The increasingly common stories of entrapment in a system that has no flexibility, and the reliance on the goodwill of strained families and friendship 'networks', mean that ill older people continue to be perceived as a miss-fitting 'problem' to be solved. *Well* older people, on the other hand, or perhaps more realistically those choosing quiet stoicism, are perceived to be 'lucky' and increasingly, particularly in the housing market, as people who are house 'blocking'. Older people who are getting on with their lives, living in houses that are deemed too big for them, are coming under some scrutiny, with building firms now providing 'solutions' by carving off 'graddy' (graduate) flats and creating retirement homes and complexes. According to the political theorists, this then encourages older people to move, and liberates housing stock for the more 'deserving' young. The hint of deserving and undeserving elderly people wafts through these discussions, and is reminiscent of the Poor-Law ideas of deserving and undeserving poor. House blocking? Bed blocking? What next? Perhaps older people should be encouraged to go out only during the day, and go on trains or buses only when the 'busy' young people are less likely to need them? Very soon we can see that we can arrive at a perfectly logical argument which says that disengagement from the mainstream is not only possible, but required. Older people can easily become service blockers or even 'good-life' blockers.

As Christians, we need to think very carefully about supporting social policies that allow the disengagement of an increasingly large section of the population from others. Social policy can easily have the effect of splitting older people into different camps, and thereby can reduce the power of any obvious collective, coherent and rational voice. The church is no stranger to dividing people into groups perceived as more or less 'useful': the recent interest taken by the Church of England in 'people with dementia' and the 'nature of the worship required' is one such division, however well-intentioned, which may prove to be extremely unhelpful in the long run, simply ghettoising older people with cognitive impairment, and creating yet another category of 'not me'.

This is partly reinforced by elders themselves who, as we saw in Chapter 1, don't want to be viewed as belonging to the stigmatised 'older-person' group. Discrimination, bad feeling and misunderstanding are always greater if we don't *know* those in the 'out' group. The less experience we have of ageing and its discontents, the more likely we are to be judgemental, fearful and dismissive of our older fellow human beings. The combination of our innate fear of ageing and a social environment where ageing is seen as a 'problem', not just for the individual but for the smooth running of society, will be and often is a toxic one. Compassion for and identification with the 'other', always in short supply, risk becoming scarcer. We need to live with each other in a state of mutual recognition of our common humanity. The warning of 'ghettos and silos' needs to be held up to our continually evolving health and social care services. And, as carers and elders, we can play our part in questioning, in breaking down barriers, in creating connections and in recognising our common destiny. Much can be achieved through recognition of our universal experience of ageing and human psychological functioning, which lets us scrutinise the politics and the social policy afresh.

Mental illness

Our societal attitudes and reactions to mental illness remain rooted in fear of the strange 'other' we cannot (or will not) understand. Mental illness remains, despite the insights gained from advances in biology and neuroscience, variously a subject for derision, horror, mirth and curiosity, hiding a deep-seated fear of loss of control. The recent London–based Wellcome Collection exhibition 'Bedlam' in 2016–17 on psychiatric service development over the last four centuries showed, among other things, how the Victorians would visit the asylums as a sort of social Sunday outing: the lurid tales, often wildly exaggerated, of disinhibited inappropriate behaviour became a source of titillation. Not much has changed, really: new types of social media simply afford different methods for the 'visiting', for the 'naming and shaming'. The 'Bedlam' exhibition also displayed a shared vision of the future created by people who had been diagnosed with a mental illness: they produced a 'designer asylum', interestingly returning to the true ideal of a place of space and safety. This shared design built in the capacity for those living in the community to indulge their eccentricities in a collective way, providing an essentially spiritual space for creativity, reflection and withdrawal.[64]

These ideas are a late modern reworking of the ideas put forward by the Quakers in the York community in 1786. The Quaker principles of justice, peace and simplicity have a deeply spiritual basis. Despite contemporary high-profile campaigns and celebrity 'confessions' to depression, dementia, bipolar disorder, personality disorder, dementia and other conditions, which have tried to 'normalise' mental disorder within a proper spectrum of mental healthiness, the social stigma around mental disorder still provides lasting difficulties for those who experience any of these phenomena. Stigma, of course, also influences the way social and healthcare policy is structured and funded: for instance, dementia in 2016 was newly seen (through changes to death certification processes) as being the biggest killer of older people, well beyond heart disease and cancer, and yet government funding of dementia-related research remains a fraction of that for cancer. As we write, the historical structural arrangements for National Health Service (NHS) funding dictate that the mental health budget remains dependent on the first-in-line 'draw' of money from acute health services, and so mental health remains a Cinderella to the ugly sisters of acute hospital services, despite its vital role. The desperate need for social care support to adjoin and alleviate the strain on our NHS is in our headlines daily: the issue of funding for social care for older frail people, particularly those with a mental illness, looms as a large and apparently insoluble problem. There are, however, glimmers of hope, with some of our more enlightened politicians beginning to understand the issues more deeply through constituents' stories.[65]

As we age, we are more susceptible to certain forms of mental illness. For example, Alzheimer's disease, uncommon in those under 50, becomes more likely thereafter. Beyond 80 years of age, our chances of having cognitive problems, particularly memory loss and behavioural change, increase exponentially. In this condition, as with others, there is an acceleration of risk as time progresses. We'll say a little more about dementia later in this chapter. Other mental disorders, for instance depression and anxiety, are also more prevalent in older age. But mental disorder does not come out of nowhere: one mistake we continue to make is to draw distinctions between physical ill health and mental ill health, as though one has no bearing on the other. In fact, the man with incurable cancer is an anxious man, if not about death, then at least about the manner of his treatment. However, this distinction is very deeply ingrained in us, and in many ways still forms the basic structure for health and social care policy, as we have seen with its public financing. Mental ill health in older people continues to be underinvestigated and undertreated. Physical health and mental health are inextricably linked, one affects the other, and to make these categorical distinctions is to miss the opportunity to give good care.

Not all agencies miss the point, of course. Years ago, the Minority Report by Peter Townsend[66] showed quite clearly the links between poverty, ageing and ill health. As one of many examples, the Centre for Ageing Better[67] makes the links between physical exercise and mental well-being, and housing and pensions and mental well-being. In fact, all the indicators of successful ageing that we listed in Chapter 3 contribute to good overall well-being, despite the presence or absence of specific illnesses.

'Cumulative trivia' and 'mild cognitive impairment': helpful concepts?

Elspeth Hockey, an Edinburgh-based academic in the late 20th century, wrote about 'cumulative trivia'.[68] This is a process in which small irritations become major dramas. It is particularly relevant to those who are increasingly frail. Her idea was that the small day-to-day 'trivial' problems of ageing can accumulate into a whole that becomes unmanageable, requires attention and is potentially life-changing, plunging the older person into an essentially unnecessary situation of dependence.

JOSEPHINE and ANGUS

Let us think a little about Angus and Josephine through this particular lens. We have seen Angus through bereavement and a second happy marriage and now he is in his 90s with a neuropathy which means he has trouble feeling and placing his feet. He has lots of help and his younger wife can manhandle him when necessary if he has wobbly moments. However, one morning, when his wife has popped out to buy a paper for him, Angus trips on a mat that is lying awkwardly and which catches his Zimmer walking aid. This causes him to stumble and wrench his wrist as he clutches the arms of the Zimmer, with no obvious harm done. He rights himself and makes it to his chair. He doesn't mention this stumble to his wife when she returns a few minutes later. It is too trivial to mention. He does mention the rug and they make sure it is well spread out, making a note to have it fixed to the floor with some tacks next time one of the children appears.

During the morning, Angus' wrist starts to hurt. This is his dominant hand: he finds he can't pick up his coffee cup so well. He spills some of his coffee on his shirt and in his effort to wipe it clean he rubs in the stain. This was a clean shirt: he and his wife are entertaining in the afternoon; friends are coming for lunch and card games. Angus would like to change his shirt because it looks a bit messy, but he doesn't want the fuss of getting a clean shirt from upstairs, or indeed having to go through the laborious process of unbuttoning and buttoning his shirt, all of which takes forever because of his neuropathy and mild sensory impairment; he doesn't like his wife doing it, because he feels that it reduces him to a child. So, he entertains in a dirty shirt; his wrist is hurting, and his concentration on the card game is less intense than his 'card sharp' reputation suggests. His friends notice his discomfort, but don't know the cause of it. They confirm with each other that Angus seems to be becoming frailer: the signals are his dirty shirt and his slightly distracted air. These are characteristics hitherto unconnected to Angus: this new identification of frailty on the part of his social group means that they then reorganise the cards-and-lunch regular event, hoping to be kind and so that Angus is not burdened with the entertaining any more.

This is a well-intended gesture, but of course effectively diminishes Angus' ability to retain his social equality with the others. They say that they will collect him from his house, with his wife, and that they will return them; this transforms the relationships subtly, and puts Angus at social disadvantage. This is felt as 'depressing' by Angus, who hardly understands but recognises a social change. He feels he cannot contribute in the way he used to, and decides to give up playing cards. He comes up with some reasons that are socially acceptable, and within a month the card group is functioning without him. They now 'visit', rather than coming to play cards. They are well-meaning and kind, but the rules of engagement have changed. Angus is frail and fading and seems rather quiet. Angus feels a bit low and mentions this to the GP at his next appointment. After some discussion, the GP prescribes an antidepressant. The medication affects Angus, making him feel sleepy and lethargic. This compounds his sense of a downward spiral. So, in one month and because of a trivial trip on a carpet, Angus becomes 'other'. He becomes, in relationship with others, 'old and frail with mental health problems'.

Then there is Josephine. As we know, Josephine's pressing and overwhelming wish to live independently at home seems to have come to nought: she is now living in the local residential and nursing home. She chooses not to leave her room or join in the 'activities'; her visitors, whilst still numerous, have subtly changed the way they relate to her. She is now a frail old lady in a nursing home. This is exactly what she predicted and feared. Her response to this is to deepen further her relationship with God. She listens to sacred music, and continues to keep up her prayer cycle. She has the prayer cycle, written in notes, beside her bed. She is virtually bedridden now, and one morning a nice cheerful young care attendant tidies up her things after bringing in a cup of tea. The care attendant doesn't know that Josephine has a prayer diary, and that access to this and to her prayer beads is essential to the structure of her day. This well-meaning young person tidies away the rather odd beads, and puts them out of Josephine's reach. She then disappears to tidy the next room.

Josephine leans over to pick them up, finds they are not to hand and rummages about under the bedclothes, assuming they have got lost somewhere in the sheets. She twists and turns to try and find them, and in doing so pulls at her urinary catheter, now permanently in place. This proves painful, and during the morning it becomes clear that Josephine needs attention. Permanent catheters are outside the care home's purview, so the district nurse from the local practice is called but is busy, so that she cannot come until the evening. Meanwhile, the positioning of the displaced catheter is very uncomfortable, and Josephine is in some pain. She has not been able to say her prayers with her beads all day, and is disconsolate. She has a visitor who is not able to find the beads either, and who cannot stay long enough for them to say prayers together.

Josephine becomes distressed, and (perhaps further stressed by age-related cognitive reserve) she rather uncharacteristically starts to shout out. And so on… we can see that one small thing leads to big changes, to erroneous assumptions and to 'frail elders with mental health problems'.

These two rather depressing scenarios repeat themselves endlessly. Trivial mishaps become major difficulties. These examples echo what used to be called the 'social causal ascription of mental illness', when we were less able to pay attention to the biological realities of brain disease, and before hopes of a cure for dementia (and other cognitive failings) were raised, perhaps prematurely and perhaps (who knows?) with many attached fantasies about what would prove clinically possible or likely. Now, as neuroscience edges forwards, we are better placed to integrate our ideas about brain pathology, and even our fervent hopes of a 'magic bullet' to come, with what we know about social functioning. However, our hopes of scientific breakthrough in no way reduce the importance of what we know about social assumptions, about decline and diminishment, about mental fragility in old age. These assumptions remain pernicious and powerful just *because* of the elements of social and psychological truth attached to them, and look unlikely to go away any time soon. There *is* diminishment in old age, and capacity *does* change. The difficulty is rooted in the *judgements* made about mental disorder, rather than by the disorder itself. Having said that, of course, some people will carry with them into their old age serious mental disorder needing medical attention. And, because of the inbuilt assumption that older people will somehow display less competence, it can often be difficult to establish clear diagnoses and to administer the appropriate treatments for specific mental illness.

This is a sensitive and complex area. When *does* Angus' mild cognitive impairment become a mental disorder that needs attention? While it can be helpful to have a diagnosis of mild cognitive impairment that can provide a label, the label itself can assume prophetic capacity, with expectations of worsening and the encouragement of catastrophic thinking, rather than of careful planning. At what point do the inevitable slips and scrapes and changes of older age *need* to become coalesced around a diagnosis? The purpose of a diagnosis is to help the diagnosed come to some understanding of their condition, and to provide as much support in various ways as might be helpful. Managing one's mental health is a big task at the best of times, and is a greater challenge as one ages and has less social power to challenge the stereotypes.

We are all, in fact, vulnerable to mental disorder (just think of poor Angus and Josephine), and this includes the spiritual carer. Having a spiritual focus is sometimes very helpful (God understands our disorders, major or minor), and developing good sincere relationships with each other can be a source of comfort and joy. However, church congregations, with their apparently spiritual focus, are as susceptible as everyone else to habitual stereotyping and distancing of older people. The laying on of particular spiritual support for older people, however well-intentioned, may or may not be helpful and needs to be carefully thought about with regard to sustaining authentic relationships.

Dementia

A public awakening to the trials of those with dementia and their carers has been championed by several high-profile examples.[69] Although this book is not about dementia-related illnesses or celebrities, it would be a mistake not to mention dementia in the general context of ageing, given its generation of fear beyond its prevalence. The cognitive symptoms that comprise the clinical picture of dementia include failures in both attention and concentration as well as in memory loss, and there is an increasing chance of these symptoms, together with behavioural disturbance, becoming manifest as we grow older. There is much written about the likely subjective experience of such cognitive loss, together with deeper consideration of the psychological and social issues we have already touched upon, and we suggest that the reader caring specifically for those with dementia looks at some particular texts for help and guidance. We particularly recommend the book by Professor John Swinton, who was awarded the Michael Ramsay theological writing prize in 2016 for this work.[70] In it, he makes the case for a more benign and compassionate understanding of dementia and a rediscovery, after Kitwood[71] (another great favourite), of the *person* who is displaying the symptoms. No two experiences and manifestations of dementia are the same, and there are incidentally many differing causes of dementia. The important thing to remember is that the *person with DEMENTIA* is a *PERSON with dementia*. This means that (like the rest of us) they will have spiritual needs and concerns, and trajectories that have had a lifetime to describe themselves. The care for the spiritual needs of people with dementia is quite as exacting, broad and unique as that of those without dementia: only the storytelling is less readily evoked. The point about spiritual need also very much applies to the care of those who are caring for people with dementia, who potentially find the burden carried one of great heaviness. We are of course all people, we all have our flaws and failings, our talents and triumphs, and our spiritual lives are uniquely experienced; we must be careful to avoid assumptions based solely on our own experiences.

There is a huge variety of activities and practices that specifically consider the spiritual care of people with dementia. There is real concern that people with particularly advanced dementia, where communication becomes more complex, need, deserve and thrive on spiritual support. Readers interested in this may like to read about the Purple Bicycle project, carried out in a selection of care-home settings. We refer to this in Chapter 10. We would reiterate that, while people with dementia have spiritual needs and while particular talents are desirable in all caregivers, the essence of good spiritual care is always to build a loving and honest relationship which allows God, our source and creator, to flow through and between each person. In this view, spiritual care is both the same for all and uniquely configured for each of us.

Disability and refocusing

In the absence of the achievement of the ambitious goal of the compression of morbidity in later life, to which we have referred earlier, the reality of increasing disability is something that we must face. We are living longer and will experience disability more and for longer; the 'suffering years' will extend, and there are some alarming statistics that suggest that, as we age, we might experience more than a decade of 'suffering' old age. Quite what that suffering entails is unknown to each of us, but it may start with small irritations and proceed to interfere with our quality of life, and our capacity for the independent activities of daily living. At this stage, we will require help either in the form of family or relatives, or paid help, to maintain our independent living status. In addition to the 'cumulative trivia' and increasing support needs, some of us will experience specific catastrophic disability, which suddenly changes our position in the world, or incremental disability, which will slowly diminish that position in the world.

At most ages, and certainly over the age of 60, any one of us, if pressed by a clinician, could cite about six or seven symptoms on any one day. Some of these symptoms would relate to each other, and some would stand alone. The 'multiple pathology' that the older person experiences is one of the huge complexities for medical and social care and treatment. We are all to some degree disabled by our ageing, in the sense that we cannot now do as easily what we could do as younger people. We are also, however, enabled and liberated to refocus on other things, to think in other ways, by these same restrictions and 'disabilities'. So, Angus is liberated from the garden he always found a chore, in favour of polishing his card-playing and jigsaw skills. The number of banal and seldom-told stories of disability leading to life enrichment vastly outweigh those stories of utter desperation. So our lives offer us *both* suffering and joy, disability and ability, containment and liberation. This is the message of the gospel and the experience of ageing. Richard Rohr discusses life's suffering journey in his various books, including *Falling Upward*.[72] Echoing Frankl, he refers to the tragic nature of life's journey with its ups and downs, its highs and lows, and the inevitable suffering along the way.

The acceptance of the reality of suffering is not a particularly happy prospect, particularly in Western cultures where Christianity has fled this territory of humility in favour of the seductive comforts of medical science, some real but many imagined. Increases in mean population age, together with relative decreases in the capacities of state care provision, mean that the noble 'carer' is increasingly engaged, willingly or otherwise. This shift comes at a time in our culture when many family members and obvious main carers live at a distance, have multiple other commitments and live in increasingly complex family structures. So, on paper and in reality, the whole ageing, disability and caring arrangement is a challenge, and one that should be pondered and discussed with 'significant others' long before a crisis occurs. Ideally, the arrangement is also the subject of ongoing refinement and alteration as things change.

The social construction of disabilities: lack of trust

Disabilities are also a matter of perception. In a society where youth, speed and physical prowess are honoured, valued and lauded, disability is seen in the negative as 'being unable to do some things that others can do, as part of being independent and capable'. This huge subject again falls outside the scope of this book, but it is worth taking a short detour just to think briefly about the consequences of the *construction of disability* for the ageing person.

If you live alone and cannot open a tin, or hold a pan, this is a disability which needs attention. Other means of feeding yourself and cooking are sought. However, 'feeling disabled' is a different phenomenon, it seems, from having a disability which requires some creative adjustment. Older people are presumptively disabled by a society that constructs itself around the assumption of specific capacities. Here is an example in the ageing trajectory of Josephine.

Josephine uses two sticks on the rare occasions when she goes out, because her balance isn't great and it makes her feel safer. She is due to go to an outpatient appointment at her local hospital. There is a good bus service and, despite her catheter, she has no need for help beyond sticks. She waits at the bus stop. The bus arrives. The driver opens the doors. Josephine embarks on the rather slow process of getting on the bus. It all takes a bit of time. She has her pass in her bag, but it is strung around her neck, so that she can manage the two sticks. In the process of climbing on board the bus, she somehow loses the opening to her bag, and must retrieve it by letting go of one stick. Retrieval takes time. The pass is found. Josephine shows it to the bus driver. The driver shuts the doors. Josephine retrieves her second stick, and makes her way into the bus. The bus, now late per tight schedule, moves off suddenly. Josephine lurches forwards and only just manages to fall into a seat. Rattled by this experience and the feelings of inadequacy it sets up in her, Josephine finds herself upset and exhausted by the time she gets to the appointment, and takes a taxi home, which is expensive, provoking and prolonging anxiety.

The next step for Josephine is to ask for hospital transport for her appointments, or to find some other means of getting to the appointments that doesn't involve the bus. Somewhere inside her, she knows that if she falls she might not be helped: she has lost her trust in her fellow human beings, but still doesn't want carers to accompany her. This lack of trust that now threatens to dominate all our moral landscapes, in big corporations and small families, is a phenomenon described by a variety of writers, including Francis Fukyama.[73] If I can trust my fellow strangers to help me, then my disabilities are less disabling. If I can't trust them to help me, then I must make contingency plans. Lack of trust in relationships raises anxiety and is a big problem. Spiritual care is all about building trusting relationships, where our fragilities are respected and supported. This applies to both carer and older person. Disability is made worse by our lack of trust.

Loss, grief and weariness

In Margaret Drabble's novel *The Dark Flood Rises*, there are several ageing characters contemplating and living out their diminishments. Fran, the main figure in the story, is active, in her 60s and working for the improvement of housing for older people, while she herself, of course, is growing older. This is a classic and familiar situation: 'Meals on Wheels' services are, not uncommonly, delivered by someone older than the recipient. The 'young-old' often work with and for the 'old-old' (and sometimes the other way around). The character Fran is described by Drabble as 'too old to die young, and too old to avoid bunions and arthritis, moles and blebs, weakening wrists, incipient but not yet treatable cataracts and encroaching weariness'. In Fran's case, she is looking after her ex-husband as he lies dying. Fran is reunited with her school friend Teresa, who interestingly is also dying, and is precariously in touch with her children, who are variously struggling their way through their middle years, with their own shares of grief and anxieties. Fran has occasion to stay with her daughter, and finds some family memorabilia in the bedroom she is using. This triggers memories, and of course attached sentiments demanding review. Margaret Drabble then writes a paragraph that touches the heart of old age and loss:

> Fran feels a great tearfulness rising up in her, a grief for all things, a grief for her daughter and thence, from that grief, a grief for all things. She had feared that she would outlive such

grief, that her heart would grow thin and cold, that grief would ebb from her as sexual hope and desire and much of her social optimism (though not yet all) had ebbed from her... She had thought that ageing would bring calm and indifference and impersonality. She knew it was unlikely to bring her peace of mind... She is, it would seem, condemned to grief, to an ever replenishing well of grief rising up from the centre of the earth of her body.[74]

It is worth unpacking this powerful extract. Fiction, particularly of the quality produced by Margaret Drabble, helps us articulate what is unspeakable for most of us. Drabble describes, through her character, that sense of overwhelming sadness for times lost and lives unlived, for opportunities not taken, for 'roads not travelled'. One grief leads to all grief. Grief, feeling a sense of deep loss and the weariness that accompanies this, is the great temptation of old age. The loss of a sense of meaning and purpose can be one outcome of grief, even if it proves temporary. Fran's school friend Teresa seems to avoid this by concentrating on her faith, and her expectations of peace, but Fran herself seems unable to do this. Not many people have Teresa's single-minded faith; most are much more like Fran. And yet the spiritual need in Fran to feel a sense of peace and calm is also, according to Drabble, 'flattening'. It may be that for some, including Fran, the experience of grief is preferable to the blandness of calm indifference and impersonality.

Grief, of course, is very close to regret. 'Time lost, time passed,' to paraphrase Eliot again. And, with minimal time ahead, how can grief convert to peace, hope and reconciliation? This is the focus of the spiritual journey into old age. The spirit can try to make something meaningful out of grief. Fran's spiritual task is to sit with the ever-replenishing well of grief, without letting it consume her. Not easy. Many writers talk about the restlessness and weariness that we experience in different moments, as we live out our life's span. St Augustine wrote about the restless spirit searching for meaning. Mark Buchanan calls it the 'groanings' that we express in our longing for things unseen.[75] There is both a positive and a negative tinge to these occasional flashes of feeling. Mark Buchanan suggests that we are 'heaven bent', by which he means that we are born with a tilt in that direction. We have eternity in our hearts somewhere, buried beneath layers of this life, and we need first to find it and then to keep in touch with it. We cannot escape this yearning, which grieves as much as it encourages us.

Suffering

It is important to spend a bit of time thinking about this. Richard Rohr gives us great encouragement in his book *Falling Upward* by his embrace and confirmation of the validity and reality of the suffering life. We must take on the ideas of suffering as central to the 'tragic' elements of our lives here on this earth. So many writers have encouraged us to do this. As we've already noted, Scott Peck in his early work *The Road Less Travelled* opens the book with the phrase, 'Life is difficult', and so it is. We are all looking and searching for ways through the inevitable suffering and difficulties we inevitably meet. Frankl writes about the tragic triad of guilt, suffering and death that confronts us all and challenges us to find meaning. We will suffer, we do suffer, we have suffered. Jesus' earthly life teaches us much of the tragedy of suffering. A man of God, who comes to preach compassion, kindness and love, is nailed up and killed, instead of a man who has murdered many, a terrorist. But, of course, the crucifixion happens to absolve not only the terrorist, but all of us. Jesus' message of hope then was seen as so outrageous and out of time, so dangerous precisely because it seemed to favour the dispossessed: he had to be brutally silenced in order to discourage others. Jesus suffered, showing us something of the inevitability of life's tragedy.

We are all born with the 'spirit of God' in us, and we can take a lifetime to retrieve it; often it is a process of 'little by little'. Rohr points out the tragic cycle of life and death in nature: both creatures and plants develop, grow and die. As human beings, we tend, and tragically need, to hold in our minds an optimism that it will be different for us, there will be no sense of crucifixion: somehow, we will escape the tragic elements of nature's dance. But, of course, we cannot: no one avoids suffering altogether. Unanumo, an Italian philosopher, writes of the way that life is not a continual progression, but a circular process of joy and sorrow, tragedy and triumph, reconciliation and distrust. In our suffering is an eternal longing to go 'home': a longing for a better place, perhaps with our long-dead mothers. This yearning or longing Rohr calls 'homesickness': something in us is calling us. This is the spirit within us: the ever-present dynamic balance between brokenness and healing is tipping, we want to go home, we are missing something. So our suffering is embedded with our yearning. We hardly know this inner process: on rare occasions, we catch glimpses of our path, our way, and then the clouds gather again. On a beautiful day, as the sun comes out, we are filled with light. The seasons mediate our suffering. Some days, things feel better than others.

As we age, our suffering persists, perhaps highlighted in certain areas: our suffering is not because we are terrible sinners, but because we are human beings. And, as we age, perhaps our yearnings increase. We have all met older people who declare themselves 'ready to go', sometimes elders, but sometimes younger people who have borne great suffering and trial. The comfort for them of the state of being in readiness is deeply uncomfortable for those who (carers or not) have not yet felt, or thought deeply about, that pull. Pity the poor elder who, in addition to their own troubles, must deal with *our* discomfort as well.

Death and dying

Paraphrasing Mark Buchanan, whose work we quoted earlier: 'We are all dying'. *'Memento mori'* (remember that you will die) was a relentless accompaniment spoken by advisors to victorious Roman generals and politicians, as in their egocentricity they soaked up adulation and praise after victory: *memento mori* served as a potent reminder of the journey into humility, decline and death inevitably awaiting them. It awaits us all. Christians are given hope, meaning and purpose in the form of Christ and his life: Christ who, through suffering, 'broke the bonds of death and set us free'. Without this idea of eternity in a better place, the whole process of life and our own suffering becomes almost absurd, given the evident extreme difficulties with which most people contend in one form or another. No system of healthcare, however well developed and funded, however sensitively psychologically informed, can get around this reality. The decline in formal religious teaching we see in this age in the West cannot surely be disassociated from the increasing reports of despair and loneliness found in social surveys and anecdotally. The idea that life is at the very least a spiritual journey gives a positive complexion to an otherwise dull trudge in semi-darkness towards pointlessness.

Death and dying are, of course in this context, deeply spiritual matters. The hospice movement has done much to promote spiritual care, and there is currently a whole range of chaplaincy responses to death and dying. Far less attention is paid in healthcare to ageing and being old; as Helen Small points out, having a philosophy of death, or feeling a need to have one, is not the same as having a philosophy of old age.[76] The Christian faith offers overlap: in many senses, attending to a *way* of death is much easier and certainly more common than attending to a *way* of being old. Now that we are going to be old longer, and probably have multiple disabilities along the way, we need to think more about the journey towards death as well as about death and dying itself.

Thinking about this journey tends to herald a change in our understanding of life, and is often part of the transition to the second half of life, where issues of the meaning and purpose of one's life, and its place in the scheme of things, become more pressing. The movement into the second half is a particular moment in our spiritual journey: this is the subject of Chapter 8.

Chapter 8

'Clouds of glory': the second half of life and its spiritual tasks

One of the chief signs of the shift into the second half of life is the move from the magical ideas of childhood through the heroic, necessary self-delusion of youth and early adulthood, to the sober experience of limitation and regret in later life. Few of us arrive at the second half of life with clarity, conviction, satisfaction, because life too often led one along a tortuous path, away from the road envisioned. I could never have envisioned what my second half of life has brought, nor could many reading this.[77]

A thing is true at first light and a lie by noon.[78]

But Jesus called the children to him and said, 'Let the children come to me and do not stop them, because the Kingdom of God belongs to such as these. Remember this! Whoever does not receive the Kingdom of God like a child will never enter it.'
LUKE 18:16–17

This chapter discusses the implications of making a conscious and intentional step into a different second half of our life. This second half must inevitably be lived differently from the first. The vicissitudes of age, discussed in a previous chapter, and the ever mobile and fluid socio-political landscape will make this so. The imperative of change, choice and journey in the second half of life provides opportunities for 'return', retrieval and review. Sometimes this is called a 'late flowering', and we can see this in discussions about the value and difference of the late work of great artists, writers and thinkers. Something changes, and our perspective shifts; we see and express the world differently.

However, this shift does not happen automatically. We don't reach midlife and suddenly become both wise and reconciled to our ageing selves. In the West, we have, as Richard Rohr notes, 'first-half-of-life' minds. These minds are dualistic, not contemplative. We are trained to see things in binary, opposing, terms; dark–light, right–wrong, black–white, up–down, good–bad, ill–well, young–old.

The work of Ian MacGilchrist in *The Master and His Emissary*[79] helps us to conceptualise two types of thinking generated within different parts of our brain. One type is very rational and logical and 'calculating'. The other is more emotional and contextual. In very crude terms, we can imagine that there are two hemispherical halves to our brain. In our current Western society, we are overusing the rational half or side, at the expense of the other half, the right side, which gives us our emotional stabilities, understandings and sensitivities. MacGilchrist suggests that there is an ultimate dysfunctionality of the neurobiology behind our overpromotion of, or overdependence on, the rational and calculating skills of our left cerebral hemisphere (the 'emissary'), without adequate attention to the spatial, emotional and contextual inputs of the right hemisphere (the 'master'). To achieve movement into life's second half, we need to give up our binary certainties. We must attend to the emotion and acknowledge the relationship between love and suffering the mysteries of life. Often, a change is triggered in us as the result of some kind of dramatic event such as major illness, the death of a loved one or some event which forces us to review and rethink ourselves and our position in the world. It is exhausting and challenging to make these changes, but only then can we step into the second half with confidence and some joy.

The 'second half' of life must be lived differently

Carl Jung, a psychiatrist grounded in clinical work among the profoundly mentally ill, saw ageing as an opportunity for serious personal spiritual investigation, and became one of the founding fathers of psychoanalytic thinking. Freud, his equally brilliant contemporary and arguably the better writer, worked clinically among the neurotic bourgeoisie of Vienna, and seemed to think ageing was of little analytic interest, a condition of decline to be avoided or perhaps denied. Freud was dismissive of the idea that anyone over the age of 50 would engage in serious self-reflection and analysis, believing that the ageing individual becomes locked into fixity of thought, whereas Jung's view seems to have been that serious review would most likely get started in midlife.

Kathleen Woodward, in her masterly work on ageing and its discontents, picks up on and re-examines Freud's distaste for old age. She notes that 'in our culture we are profoundly ambivalent and primarily negative about old age'.[80] She confirms that the predominant view of ageing is as undesirable, based on evidence from literary works, using psychoanalytic concepts to think about ageing. In Freud's work and influence she finds a powerful anti-age sentiment that runs on as a strong theme through the 20th and 21st centuries, only really being challenged as the demographic reality starts to have an impact. More elders, more ageing experience, more pressure on social and medical services: finally, emergent within our narcissistic culture and despite the taboos, there is a dawning gleam of realisation that ageing happens to us all.

Jung, on the other hand, is very positive about ageing. He offers the idea of a 'second half of life' that brings with it a complete overhaul, a requirement to look at the world and oneself afresh. This is in sharp distinction to the idea that midlife values and practices should be maintained if possible into old age, the latter idea being one that commonly prevails in the gerontological literature, and which is reflected in the '*vox pop*' about ageing. The popular press and social media promote the simple idea of *capacity*, and adherence to the glory days of the past: we are still able to do things associated with young people, or that we did in our own young lives. In some ways, this is useful; we discuss the relationship between continuity and change in greater detail in our chapter on retirement, but one simple fact should stand out for us here: as we age, we change.

Jung focused on the opportunities for change in the psyche, as we grow older and recognise ourselves as ageing. We start to interpret familiar things differently. Jung puts it memorably, and perhaps more gently than Hemingway:

> We cannot live the afternoon of life according to the programme of life's morning; for what was great in the morning will be little by evening, and what in the morning was true will at evening have become a lie.[81]

The understanding of this is all around us, but rarely discussed in any detail. For example, if you look at humorous birthday cards that are aimed at teasing those who are ageing, the tensions between remaining the same and embracing ageing are all there. The natural longing to be younger again, and the acknowledgement of changes that happen to us all, are represented. These cards make us smile or laugh just *because* they hit a nerve: they uncover a truth that some things cannot remain the same and, in some ways, acknowledge our hopes and fears about ageing.

What is change – what is the 'second half'?

The idea of change, of looking at things afresh, of seeing the same things differently, is hardly unfamiliar in a Christian context. T.S. Eliot writes at the end of his *Four Quartets* about our explorations taking us back to the same place, which helps us see things as if for the first time. We ought, as Christians, to be able to manage the ideas of constant change and the cycle of life. Renewal, resurrection, transformation, repentance and review are all part of the cycle of Christian life, just as conception, birth, growth, decline and death are features of nature and of our biology. We certainly mark the cycles of our years with the Annunciation, the Visitation, Lent, Easter, Ascension, Advent, Christmas and Epiphany. But our reactions to change tend to be complex: we like and need stability, routine, continuity. These are important anchors in our lives. 'No routines' more often suggests chaos than it implies openness to change.

In our endless search for freedom and individualism, we miss the point that freedom emerges out of discipline and constraint, just as it did for our forebears. We can see this expressed in the life of the Israelites in Egypt, and in the lives of early Christian monastics and nuns, as well as in the lives of Buddhists, monks, Hindu aesthetes and Stylites. The idea that enclosure, routine and discipline give freedom is an ancient one, and fundamental to the monastic life: 'become free by being chained'; the hostage story is often one of a sense of freedom in captivity, with Paul providing an obvious example of this.

In the preface to his book *God in All Things*, Gerard Hughes raises some difficult questions about the changing landscape of Christianity and its response to profound societal change in the last half century.[82] Writing in 2003, he notes that 'Christianity today has reached the most critical moment in its history... The institutions, forms and structures that served us well in earlier centuries no longer answer the needs of our day. Church and state are shaken and confused.' Our point here is that, just as we must reflect and grow as individuals, the church must also change and review. Jung's ideas of life's 'second half' are valid for individuals, groups *and* institutions (indeed, Jung finds the courage to apply these ideas to God himself, in *Answer to Job*).

One problem is that we don't even know when the chronological second half starts (or, indeed, if it can reasonably be seen in terms of chronology). We agonise about whether 60 is the new 40 – when are we middle-aged, when do we consider our descent into dotage to have begun, how do we *know*?

In truth, it probably doesn't matter, and it is probably very variable. The point is that at some moment in life's trajectory there will be an opportunity for change, for seeing the world differently, and that this opportunity should be anticipated and taken. Refusal, denial or postponement makes ageing otherwise very much more difficult.

Many people never manage to take the step into the second half, or do so only half-heartedly, reluctantly teetering on the edge of a psychological abyss, fearful of the jump across the chasm. The movement into the second half requires a significant shift in existing patterns of thinking. This is a spiritual matter. It is a change in perspective or an alteration of the position of the individual in the world, and in relationship to the world. In the second half of life, we do, see and know things differently; there is no going back. We can no longer see things in a 'first–half' way, once we have seen them in a 'second–half' way. Czesław Miłosz, Nobel laureate, wrote about provinces of life, as we have already seen, and the new province of old age, where not much is known about that country 'til we land there ourselves with no right to return'. This leaves us being careful of our relationships with those who are in a different 'half', particularly peers who may choose to cling to 'first-half' ideas and values. We return to this idea in Chapter 9, when we consider opportunities provided by retirement. Here, we would emphasise that there is a difference between being forced into a realisation of old age, being a reluctant tourist eager to return 'home', and being an adventurous traveller, eager to understand the culture of the new land, to learn the language and to enjoy the new fruits.

David Ogston, who was a minister in the Church of Scotland, was a particularly talented, brilliant writer, broadcaster and preacher of the gospel. We have already mentioned him in the introduction to this book. After his very early death at 63, his friend Johnston McKay and his wife, Meg, sorted through his papers, producing two endlessly valuable compendia of his writings, one based on Lent and the other on Advent. In his Lenten musings, David writes about the moment in his life when he was propelled into realising that things had to change. He became ill. His was a sudden displacement; he writes of presiding at Holy Communion when he suddenly felt unable to continue, as though his body was not connected to the ground. Away from work, he recovered over a period of months, and during that process began, he says, to see the world differently. He talks in his writings about opening his eyes to other possibilities; there seems little doubt that, using his existing considerable talents and gifts, he made a new life for himself and his family that mined different aspects of his personality, and different interpretations of his skills. In his writing, he reviews and retrieves aspects of his being that had been lost. He finds himself remembering his father in much more detail than before. He writes about rediscovering and retrieving his lost child-self, of slowly and gradually recognising this child, as he learns again to garden and to sew. The power of creativity, something to which we will return, helps David to make the changes that he needs to make to continue his journey. David becomes an adventurous spiritual traveller, courageous enough to let go of some of his security anchors.

As carers of older people or as ageing individuals, or indeed often as we occupy both those roles, we too must become adventurous travellers, and remember that we have a sublime companion in Christ. Particularly in our caring for others, we need to take care to avoid being impediments to their progress. Jesus warned us about this when he said, 'Suffer the little children.'

Learning from children

In a very interesting study about children and spirituality, David Hay and Rebecca Nye pursue the idea that very young children have an innate spirituality, which means that they recognise mystery, wonder and the sacred unseen.[83] David Hay was continuing the zoologist Alastair Hardy's lifelong exploration of natural or biological spirituality. Children, less obviously 'cerebral' than adults, are tuned in to the bodily self, the mother earth, the wonders of the heavens, and they accept the mystery of life in a way of wonder that most adults cannot, or have forgotten. It seems that (in the West at any rate) the child is 'taught' to see things in a certain way, a process that we call 'growing up'. The child is gradually told that the mysterious, the unknown and the magical are childish things that should be put away; things that do not apply in the adult world, which is of course the child's destiny. Hay and Nye hypothesised (after Hardy's *Biology of the Human Spirit*) that children have an innate understanding of the spiritual, of emotion and mood, and that this is educated out of them as they grow. This is a rather uncomfortable and confusing reminder of Paul's letter to the Corinthians (1 Corinthians 13). Here is Paul extolling the key virtue of love as bearing all things, believing all things, hoping all things, which sounds very like the kind of approach a child takes to the world, and yet, in the middle of this passage, he suddenly and somewhat incongruously says that 'when [he] grew to be a man [he] put away childish things'. Whether he sees this as a good thing or as a problem is difficult to tell, but there is an unmistakeable hint of lament.

Childhood innocence, being an adult and creative reach

Childhood wonder and natural spirituality are, of course, to be found widespread in works of literature, poetry and art. The innocence of childhood is inevitably replaced with the knowledge and experience of adulthood. The assumption of innocence and the acceptance of the replacement of innocence with 'knowing' and 'fallen-ness' is largely uncontested, and forms the basis of the theories of human development to which we have referred earlier. Innocence as an early presence in the young child, and its regrettable but inevitable departure as part of life's journey, moves the individual on into the dangerous forest of many a myth and fairy tale representing adult life, where the road is peppered with many traps. There are implications for us that, somehow, innocence is replaced by insight into adult motivations, and that with the loss of innocence comes the difficulty of temptation.

The regret expressed in Wordsworth's intimations of immortality is evident in the resonance of the opening words: 'There was a time...' His lament 'that the things which I have seen, I now can see no more'[84] can sometimes be almost unbearable for the ageing soul. However, it may be that, later, ageing can include a return to the 'clouds of glory' that trail from children as they come from God. Ageing could be a process of retrieving that wonder, perhaps some form of adult 'reaching back' or return to those 'clouds of glory', to be found in creativity in one of its very many forms. Exercising creativity lifts the spirit. Very many of us find solace and satisfaction in painting, writing, arranging flowers, sewing and gardening, but creativity can be as simple and as complex as doing a jigsaw or the construction of new (or resurrection of old) networks of personal relationship. Perhaps this is one thing we can take out of Paul's writings. This allows us, rather than sinking into childish simplicity or self-pity, to re-enter the world of wonder and spirit in a mature and thoughtful way, 'as a (wo)man' with all the years of experience, disappointment, skill and hope that we have accumulated. A mature return to one's childlike characteristics and visions seems to be what the second half of life might offer. It is a journey not to be taken lightly, but it is a journey of reward, and offers *mutuality*, opportunities for others to help (and be helped) on the way. For those of us in our later life offering care to others, the practical implications are obvious.

The 'infantilising' of older people

Another important point for those who care for older people, particularly for those elders who are very frail and who need to be fed, washed, turned, exercised and entertained, is that these people are vulnerable to being treated like children, not so much as the innocents of early childhood in our previous section, but as we remember babies being: in need of very basic mothering and what services call 'all care'. Indeed, the 'return to second childhood' is commonly misunderstood by the adult group charged with meeting their needs, whether they are government, professional carers, taxpayers or family. Rather than the positive lens of creativity with its possibilities, here a more practical and gritty realism necessarily prevails.

As we hinted in Chapter 2 when talking about different maturities of mindset, the characters of vulnerable and frail older people, whether in the minds of family or caring professional, can too readily be reduced to stereotypes of 'naughty or nice'. The life's journey endured by an elder, in which no doubt they have suffered and fully lived, can readily be swept away in a tide of soppy infantilisation or overfamiliarity, typified by unsolicited use of a Christian name which, in an earlier time, might have elicited a withering response. This, of course, can make life immediately easier for the would-be 'infantiliser', but is arguably a misuse of positional power and quite unethical. Infantilisation makes the journey immeasurably harder for the older person: it is very hard emotional work for the older adult to maintain their dignity in this overwhelming context.

Reconciliation and restitution

As we discussed in Chapter 2, the importance of early love and attachment for the individual reverberates throughout the journey of life. The experience of poor attachment and lack of love has profound implications for the person as they struggle and suffer life's inevitable slings and arrows. The second half of life beckons us into something different, where we can start to see the world differently and do things differently. We have the chance to repair and recover. This is a journey of hope. There are opportunities for review, repair, reconciliation and restitution.

Sarah Hills, in her thoughtful doctoral thesis, looks at the idea of reconciliation in the context of South African politics.[85] Political reconciliation might not seem entirely relevant to our topic here, but let's consider Hills' work in a bit more detail. She is interested in the way in which restitution must be, and is, part of the reconciliation journey, and she investigates this empirically by focusing on one process of reconciliation in Worcester, near Cape Town in South Africa. This town suffered the explosion of a bomb planted by white supremacists, which killed four and injured 69 people. It is illuminating to make some comparisons between the journey of reconciliation taken by the people of Worcester and the journey into the second half of life as experienced by older people and, in particular, the very old living in residential care.

Typically, and certainly in law, a definition of restitution is as a one-way process of the injured receiving something from the injurer; restitution means that someone makes something right again, usually by the restoring of a thing to its proper owner. Hills' redefinition of restitution is that it is in fact *two-way*, that it benefits both parties and that there are elements of equality inherent in the relationship, between the bomber and the bombed in this case. Restitution is a process that supports reconciliation. Reconciliation is both a means and an end. True restitution involves a relationship between individuals. Restitution cannot be made in isolation. Because of restitution, all parties involved feel better, even though things cannot be 'restored' to what they were before. So, restitution in this sense implies that things will and must change, but this can happen within a context of acceptance and grace. There is a sense of 'Ubuntu' about restitution, meaning, '*Without you I cannot be me*', or '*I am as I am because you are as you are*'. For restitution to be a real endeavour, both parties in the process need to feel that they play a part.

The spiritual carer, loving friend or relative of the ageing person can be supportive by encouraging reconciliation to their current ageing situation, and to their ageing self. This helps the ageing person on their journey towards integration, wholeness and hope, rather than despair and disintegration. The developmental journey into ageing discussed in Chapter 2 provides the common theme of finding hopeful balance through meeting challenge and developing creativity. Ageing involves reflection and change, in the midlife and beyond. The idea of reconciliation and restitution fits well with the ageing journey.

However, reconciliation is always partial, and restitution makes it as good as it can be. Restitution, returning grace, is found in the small acts of day-to-day life which express the relationships between the carer and the older person. The small acts can involve help with washing, eating, walking, moving, sleeping. As we age, the simple activities of daily living can become the real focus of real life, and the purpose of the day. The way in which these daily tasks are supported and understood by the carer and the ageing person can make them sacramental. So the ageing person finds a way of reconciling themselves to their ageing journey and a way to change their perspective; that has an impact on family and friends. Its noble aim is the coming to terms with the realities of ageing and death. Since the losses experienced because of ageing (in particular, moving into extreme old age) are not reversible, the restitutive acts become symbolic, partial and expressed through relationship. By providing encouragement in the simple daily acts of living, the carer can help the cared-for to move away from despair in old age and its vicissitudes, and on into something more hopeful and lighter. Reconciliation through restitutive practices of returning grace helps older people and younger people challenge together the vicissitudes of old age, and to transcend and transform these ageing experiences. So, while reconciliation can be seen as part of the work of the ageing person, and part of the spiritual care needed, Hills shows us that, for reconciliation to be most effective, it must be accompanied to some extent by restitution, and that restitution implies change.

The spiritual tasks of the second half of life: reconciling to age

We said earlier that Carl Jung, arguably one founding father of contemporary psychoanalytic thinking, was (in contrast with his early mentor Sigmund Freud) fundamentally *interested* in ageing. Jung noted that, for the ageing person, 'it is a duty and necessity to devote serious attention to himself'. In his writings, it is possible to discern a view that there are *tasks* of ageing which, if addressed, can help the ageing soul maximise the gains from this stage of life. (This work reminds us strongly of the 'challenges' presented by Erikson, a contemporary of Jung's writing from a perspective outside formal psychiatry.) Jung proposes tasks of ageing and, from a perspective of clinical psychiatric practice and much personal reflection, in short, once again suggests that the second half of life gives us a real opportunity to do things differently.

He gives us a set of quite practical tasks that help us with this:

- To face the reality of age and death.
- To review and reflect and sum up one's life.
- To find meaning through memory and analysis.
- To overcome one's ego.
- To rediscover God in oneself.
- To be creative and playful.
- To draw some mental boundaries.
- To preserve one's energies.

We'll now look at these in more critical detail. We have combined or linked some of these tasks as we examine them here. They may not be exactly as Jung intended, but his general headings are helpful jumping-off points, and have resonance with the activities of life's second half.

Facing the reality of ageing and death

Richard Rohr writes about the word 'forbearance'. This is a word, he suggests, that we rarely use in the West. Forbearance means suffering with love and for love, and suffering with and for reality. Despite our general abandonment of its use, it appears in its definitional essence as a 'gift of the Spirit' in Ephesians 5. This is the deepest meaning of passion, *patior*, which means 'to suffer and undergo reality, to allow, to acquiesce, to submit to reality'. So, as Christ submitted to his death, we are asked to submit, acquiesce and allow *this reality of ageing*. Whether or not Jung intended this particular interpretation of his task, it has resonance for those wanting to explore a 'second half' of life.

This is hard. Very few of us like the idea of ageing, and certainly even fewer of us like the idea of death. We think it is useful to separate them out, even though one generally leads to the other. Slowly and inevitably, we start to think about our own ageing, even if just to reject it. We start to see our mother's hands at the end of our arms, and our mother's face in the mirror in the morning. We begin to see that we are growing older.

Harriet writes: I clearly remember my father, to whom this book is dedicated, in this context. He was a big, handsome, very fit man. We used to holiday in a lochside cottage in the hills of the west of Scotland: we always arrived by train, then rowing boat, and there was a gate that led to the cottage. Dad always jumped over that gate, seemingly as part of his joy and celebration of being on holiday, away from the city. Perhaps I was eight. I remember clearly the first year he didn't jump over it. I wanted him to, herald as it was of his movement into 'holiday Dad', such good fun and so relaxed. I pointed out that he didn't jump over the gate. 'I couldn't do that any more,' he said. As a young girl, I wondered how he knew, without trying. As an older woman now, I know. Something in our body tells us to do things differently.

Ageing presents us with a slow and encroaching sense of change, of both physical diminishment and psychological change. It won't matter how many gym memberships are taken out, how many miles are run or how many diets are begun, the physical changes in the ageing body cannot be denied for ever. Ageing is an embodied process and, one way or the other, it happens.

Going with the ageing body, maintaining it as best we can and paying sensible attention to what can be done, is obviously good advice and of course it fills many pages of many magazines and papers, as well as countless TV programmes. What to eat, how to dress, which exercises to perform, how to stay young and fit are the staple diet of the media directed at an ageing population. However, the facing of the reality of one's own ageing, and the embracing of the change and diminishment accompanying it, are part of the journey and spiritual maturation that invite us.

We make it hard on ourselves and on each other. Competitive 'non-ageing' is an important part of the commercial marketing emphasis for the ageing population. To feel good about ourselves, it seems, there must be others who are ageing worse than we are. Some people bravely say that they are happy to look their age, but when we see them portrayed in the media, they seem to look very *unlike* how we are in the early morning! Jung's task encourages us to pay attention to our ageing in terms of accepting it, working with it and not turning it into a dreadful secret that everybody knows and nobody will acknowledge. We can help each other in this task by talking about and acknowledging our own fears and anxieties about our ageing bodies, and by reaching fewer superficial judgements based on appearance as a proxy for virtue: this is, of course, nonsense.

The small matter of death

John Dempster, writing for the *Highland Weekly News* in Scotland, noted:

I have found a couple of things I've learned recently very helpful. I suppose I'd read psychologists' views of our 'attachments' and 'aversions' before, but until recently hadn't understood how these words might apply in my own life. In my understanding, 'attachments' are things we think we need, and must have – such as possessions, or status, career or influence. 'Aversions' are the things we are afraid of, strongly dislike, view as threats. We throw all our energies into pursuing our attachments and resisting our aversions. I believe that the last and greatest 'aversion' is death, but I believe also that if we have found our identity and our security in God, then we need not fear dying, because we realise that through death, as in life, we are sustained by the Father who loves us.[86]

Not everybody easily finds this comfort of overcoming their fear of death through faith. This task is a serious challenge. It means first facing up to the idea of our death, which none of us finds easy. We know, for instance, that more than half of all adults in Britain die without writing a will – this seems to be a sure sign of denial. Nor are we any better at writing powers of attorney, so that our wishes can be made explicit and easily respected in the event of our incapacity. Jung's contribution was to understand and promote the true perception of reality, and one of life's great realities is the certainty of our death. However, T.S. Eliot famously reminds us that people cannot bear too much reality.

As we approach our 50s and 60s, death as a reality becomes more evident. Friends begin to fall ill, and some of them die. These are people 'like us', and yet they are not like us, simply because they are dead. Paul exhorts us to put aside our worldly 'eyes' and not worry about worldly matters, to keep our eyes on the main prize, which is eternal life within the Trinity. Given the circumstances in which most of us live, this is a hard 'ask'. We are surrounded and even bombarded with worldly exhortations about worldly matters of life.

David Wolfe, who died in 2011, was interested in ageing and marketing, writing a book and a blog until his death.[87] Writings under a heading of marketing seem unlikely places to gain insights about facing one's own death. However, he wrote about the achievement of *agelessness*, which was gained through accomplishing (or attempting to accomplish) Jung's tasks; being ageless for Wolfe is defined by adhering to a set of values or perhaps virtues and principles of living, rather than of transiting life stages. He suggested that the successful addressing of one's own mortality allows movement to a situation where each day is lived for its own value, and where one's life is recalibrated so that each day is mined for its adherence to and reflection of core values. So accepting our own inevitable decline and death liberates us to get on with living full lives in the present. We worry less about the future, and pay more attention to the present. This is, of course, part of the 'sufficient unto the day' of the Sermon on the Mount (Matthew 6:34, KJV). We should try not to store up treasures, for in doing so we miss the point of the wonders of the everyday. Wolfe's idea that we can become ageless if we have dealt with the reality of our death (and the fear it generates) is compelling: simply *claiming* to be ageless can be a screen for denying one's ageing self and its very real needs.

Both Josephine and Angus have had to struggle with the reality of ageing and death. By seeing his wife die, Angus is reminded of his own mortality. In her missionary work, Josephine knows both the fragility of life and its tenacity. Angus is fearful of being alone. His renewed vigour with a new love helps him put his fears back into proportion; however, age continues to beckon, pull and push, and he becomes, astonishingly to him, 90 years old. Josephine has given her own death more thought, in many ways: while living her life to the full, focusing on the detail of every day, she has tried to make daily life a sacrament. She is never the less mindful of her situation of decline: in her extreme old age, she bats back to her carers their trite assurances and platitudes. Angus, in his own extreme and extrovert old age, perhaps would welcome these.

Each person is *different*. Helping people with the practicalities of ageing and preparation for death is, arguably, fundamentally a spiritual task.

Reviewing, reflecting and summing up life: finding meaning through remembering and thinking

In whatever context we adopt it, whether as Buddhist meditation, in education or in clinical practice, the three tasks of review, reflection and summary are fundamental to any analytic position. We hold that understanding our past, and being able to tell the story of our past, are part of being able to live in the present and the future. Storytelling has become a focus of many interventions, particularly for people with memory impairment. The idea of storytelling as a means of knowing who we were, where we came from and who we now are is part of the essence of being human.

Steve Aisthorpe reminds us that there is a danger of focusing on a single story, and thereby slipping into stereotypes and prejudices.[88] We have seen that he refers to the Nigerian novelist Chimamanda Ngozi Adichie, who talks about the danger of the single story: 'Show a people as one thing, only one thing, over and over again, and that is what they become. The single story robs people of their dignity.'

This can be true of the ageing self. Without a story that is rich and multifaceted, there is an assumption that the ageing person is unidimensional, defined simply by their age and their ageing appearance. Being aware of our own multifaceted story, and reviewing it in the light of our ageing self, is part of a fruitful process of reconciliation. Telling stories, telling our story, is central to the second half of life. Stories are the secret reservoir of values, as Ben Okri wrote in 2000. He went on to say that if you change the story, you change the individual and the perception of the individual: 'If they tell themselves stories that face their own truth, they will free their histories for future flowerings.'[89] As we age, we tell more stories. Sometimes we tell the same stories that sound different in different contexts. We use stories to help us explain our lives. Joan Chittister notes that stories guide us out of the past and into a better future.[90] Jung encourages us to review our lives, to sum up and to use that review to understand ourselves more fully. Life review can be, and indeed should be, a critical look at ourselves in our own contexts. It is a process of reconciliation and restoration, and gives opportunities for change.

There is much general encouragement now to review and reflect. Memoir is a very popular form of writing, as is the idea of writing daily notes or keeping a journal. Memory groups and reminiscence work are a popular part of the toolkit of health and social care professionals working with older people. It is important to be careful not to make this a simplistic account of who someone 'used to be'; rather, to take the past into the present and the future. As we have noted earlier, James Hillman talks about improving our biographies. This means the purpose of review is to create an understanding that will help us in the future. This is an important part of being human and of ageing well.

Angus flirted with the process after his first wife's death. He made a personal journey, although he didn't necessarily see it like this, where he drove by car to all the important past places in his life, visited old friends and rediscovered his love for jazz and early music. Josephine used a daily process of reflection and review through prayer to tell her stories.

Overcoming ego and rediscovering God in oneself

This is a lifelong task, and is linked to the idea of giving oneself up to God. In more contemporary language, this may mean 'it's not all about YOU!': we may need to move beyond this barrier of its being all about us in the second half of life. Working on loving your neighbour, and on being more interested in other people than in yourself, is a difficult task, which demands creativity and imagination.

Angus was a great storyteller. He told good jokes, and was always interesting and engaging. He started, after his wife's death, to look through papers and poems that he had written. He had really forgotten all about these, and became absorbed in the way they illuminated and shed light on past thoughts. He was able to discuss these in part with his children, but mostly with his new wife. His opportunity to review and reflect was greatly enhanced with this new expression of love. Not everyone is so fortunate. The opportunity to tell one's story (to somebody who wants to hear it) in an unstructured and spontaneous way is a great blessing. Josephine has had less opportunity to rehearse her life and to share her stories with a beloved. She has, however, used her notebooks and her prayer life to reflect. She has learnt that giving snippets of her full and unusual life to the busy, hard-pressed staff simply encouraged stereotyping, particularly when staff turnover increased, and when her cultural assumptions were less often recognised. Gradually, she preferred to be more silent and chose to expect less.

In the first half, finding purpose and meaning is all about building a place in the world for oneself that is secure and safe. It is often about finding what we enjoy, about almost *literally* building a tower, home or place of safety, about creating our defences. This is essential work in the second half of life, but less literally than metaphorically, for usually we will have at least some material security. If we were given to understand in the first half of life that absolutely all our material gain would have to go in the second half, we would be defeated and demoralised before we started. So in the first half we are, overall, protected from the temptation to meaninglessness and doubt by our certainties, and to some extent by our denial of and disdain for the experience of our elders. Anybody reading this who is a parent knows that there comes a moment when advice and guidance become irrelevant, and youth will fly. We learn to be careful with our counsel, our 'guidance', in the second half of life, humbly knowing that we can only point out the very general direction of travel.

To overcome the necessary egotism of the first half, we need to settle down into a discussion with God, the creator. Our image of God can now safely change as we grow: farewell to the old, white-bearded, cloud-seated God of our childhood and ego-boundedness, so often at our beck and call when things went smoothly. This God has listened to specific instructions (prayers) about what we require, has accepted reprimands and disbelief when prayers are not answered, has become irritated and fed up with us and our nonsense. Later, as we try to move into the second half of our life, we allow our God to change. Instead of expressing relief, this God laughs, loudly and long, to the point of tears. Of course, it is not God doing the changing here, but us – although there is a view that God does change, and some who carefully unpick the theology of these ideas. In any event, God is always willingly waiting for us to pay attention, so that our relationship with him can grow. He will wait patiently, eternally for us to turn our anxious gaze from ourselves to the bigger world and universe, to the creator and creation.

Being creative and playful: creating boundaries and being wise with our energies

The subtlest of changes can help to bend the outward journey towards home, and to rediscover the inner self. Creativity does not mean that we all must become artists, painters or musicians, but it does mean that we can rediscover our playful selves. Somewhere in the fogs of time, before work, school, parents, education, financial pressures, parenting and survival took over, there was an uncluttered, creative self. This creative self uses imagination, tells stories, delights in the beauty of simple things and creates beauty and harmony for its own sake. Our *capacity to create*: this is what we need to rediscover, as we begin our rebalancing.

Angus found new creativity in his rediscovered love of jazz, and in his enduring love of early polyphony. He delighted in listening to concerts on the radio and on his renovated sound system. In good health, with kind friends, his later years were dominated by this delight in music. He found new people to share this as old friends died, and although his image of God rather doggedly remained that of an old man on a cloud, there were some enlightened moments for him, where love abounded.

For Josephine, her adherence to a timetable for her devotions and her reinforcement of those devotions throughout life gave her the freedom to enjoy both company and solitude. Her understanding of God deepened as she creatively managed her disabilities, and drew on her memories. Did the different approaches of these two elders matter: was one right, one wrong? Josephine pursued the more self-conscious awareness of her changing, deepening relationship with God, the creator; for Angus, the love he discovered in a second marriage, an expression of God's enduring love for him, meant that he gave thanks in his whole attitude to the world and his surroundings. A constant attitude in Angus' later years was one of bewildered thanks, gratitude and humility at his good fortune. Each, in their way, made these 'second-half-of-life' changes, allowing them to remain hopeful and to see a meaning for themselves. By each of them, time was used differently; but used it was, not simply endured or spent. As they grew into the second half of their life, these two continued to discern what was immediately important to them, and to focus their energies on these things. They may or may not have done this consciously, but the result was to rediscover meaning and hope.

Using the idea of spiritual tasks in day-to-day life

These tasks are not a checklist, but a series of practices to think about in the effort to move with meaning into a second half. The tasks are complex and demanding. They are summed up as a need to find a balance, and to recalibrate oneself as one enters the second half of life. Where this transition exactly falls depends on the individual and their social context, but at some stage we all start to wonder what life is about, and what it ultimately means. In the film *Jackie* (about the life of Jacqueline Bouvier Kennedy Onassis), the priest (played by the late John Hurt) advises Jackie during her extreme grief following John F. Kennedy's death, saying that every soul under heaven has times when, after they have turned out the light in the evening and are lying in bed, they wonder about their purpose and meaning. As we grow older, we begin to accept that there are no certain answers to these questions. Our purpose and meaning *are* the ultimate question, the existential question, and these tasks help us address this question.

There is an increasing interest in both the spiritual tasks of ageing and the accompanying spiritual care required by older people. Elizabeth MacKinlay published a model of spiritual tasks of ageing, where she puts centrally the task of finding meaning in our lives through searching for hope, final meaning, intimacy with God and others, and through transcending loss and disability.[91] The idea of transcending the vicissitudes of old age is contemplated by Teilhard de Chardin, who reflects on the importance of struggle against diminishment, and the redemptive nature of the struggle. This is the way we lose ourselves to God, rather than remaining wedded to our ego and worldly matters. Our journey towards God implies a loss of ego. Harold Koenig also writes extensively and specifically about the Christian spiritual needs as we age, which turn into the spiritual care tasks.[92]

This finding of balance in meaning is the most important process, the fundamental task. The balance is *always* precarious, and it requires creative imagination. The balance between work and play, between self and others, between rest and energy, between greed and abstinence, between roles, responsibilities and freedoms, between imagination and boundaries: all these are internal *and* external processes and are daily, hourly and continuous practices. This is the spiritual journey.

Above all, as we age, we look for meaning. Jonathan Sacks gives us much food for thought in his book *Not in God's Name*.[93] Once again, his book is not specifically about ageing, but there are some useful points. He suggests that there is a relationship between secularisation and loss of meaning-making skills. This is an important point for the self. Like Richard Rohr, the former Chief Rabbi talks about the insidious nature of dualistic thinking, which is encouraged by individualism. Individualism, he argues, encourages extreme views, because collective moral identity (founded on a concept of God) is absent or challenged. Those in the second half of life perhaps have a duty and a role to challenge extreme rationalism, and to remysticise life. Again, the dualistic understanding of God is that there is an external judge and father, who gives a moral code, rather than an evolving internal creator, who is and longs to be in relationship with each of us as we age. The internal conflict between youth (the young me) and age (the old me) can sometimes be unbearable. Ageing people can be angry, frightened and lost and they can project this anger on to 'youth' or care staff, doctors or children.

Perhaps the greatest life task is to become our real selves. As Jacob wrestles with the angel, and wrestles with his desire to be his brother, he realises that it is all right to be himself. The challenge is the *wrestle*, to become who we really are; to return to the 'clouds of glory' trailing so abundantly from us in early life and now all packed up in a storage box and put away under the bed. Only once that blessing of our real name or personhood is secured can we move on to optimising our ageing journey. Once we know who we are, we can move on. Retirement is one part of that reset or of doing things differently.

Chapter 9

Retirement: doing things differently

Thoroughly unprepared, we take the step into the afternoon of life. Worse still, we take this step with the presupposition that our truths and our ideals will serve us hitherto. But we cannot live the afternoon of life according to the programme of life's morning. For what was great in the morning will be little at evening, and what in the morning was true, at evening will have become a lie.[94]

The Protestant work ethic, the Calvinist work ethic or the Puritan work ethic is a concept in theology, sociology, economics and history which emphasises that hard work, discipline and frugality result in and are a sign of a person's salvation.

A person does not need to be religious in order to follow or be affected by the Protestant work ethic, as it is ingrained in certain cultures impacted by the Protestant Reformation. Worldly success is a sign of eternal salvation.[95]

This short chapter takes us towards the end of the book and the final chapter, where we will bring together some themes and look at some of the practices of our own ageing and caring. This will help our own individual spiritual development and soul journey as well as acting as the basis for the spiritual care of others as they age.

At a recent Quiet Day, we met a woman with whom we immediately connected, the way it sometimes happens. It turned out that Susan had recently retired, and she and her husband had moved into the area. She had been a teacher. In the course of our conversation, she told us that she had been on a retirement course which she had found very helpful, although she hadn't realised just quite how helpful until her husband had joined her in retirement. The retirement course leader had said to her that this moment in life was one where the relationship between the retired and the beloved had to change, and be renegotiated. This one piece of information had sustained her through some tough subsequent renegotiations. She will not be alone in this!

Retirement is certainly a process of renegotiation of self with the world, which includes close beloved relationships, but these renegotiations extend to the housework, shopping, garden, transport, activities, children and so on. To capitalise on the joys of retirement, a complete rethink is required. Walter Brueggemann's ideas help us think about this as a circular, progressive and eternal process of orientation, disorientation and reorientation.[96] This idea of constantly reviewing, discovering being confused and then finding a new way of seeing is important to our ageing story.

Retirement is one of the embarkation points for the tasks of ageing. Retirement is an obvious moment of either willing or enforced change.

One danger of retirement is in getting trapped in the morally loaded expectations that are implicit in societal institutions, in particular of health and social care, family and religion. The spiritual journey can be misunderstood as meaning *more* service, *more* unpaid work, *more* sacrifice, *more* effort. The Protestant ethic prefacing this chapter runs very deep in our society. This means that, in retirement, the individual sacred self can be sidelined and sometimes denied for the 'good of others' and in so doing misses the point of continual change and growth. For some, this feels comfortable; for others, it becomes another set of chains and restricts the possibilities of spiritual growth. The other extreme in retirement is to render oneself distant from the mainstream, to 'put up one's feet' and shut the door to the world, to such an extent that one's spiritual self gets no stimulus or food. Either way, retirement is always an opportunity for making changes, an orientation point.

We come to a change in our working life in one way or another, and these changes require us to think about ourselves and our place in the world. Currently there is an emphasis on continuation, carrying on working, being firmly located in the first half, where we contribute productively and feel good about it. This is partly prompted by the austere global financial situation since 2008, where pensions are vulnerable and less generous, and this is coupled with the expectation of longer life. This has shifted our thinking about retirement.

Current attitudes to retirement

We are relentlessly assailed with the glories of the first half of life in all forms of media. The arc-like trajectory of life, already referred to, where the pinnacle of the mid-years gives way to the decrepitude of the later years, is very much seared into our Western minds, as we have seen. It is hard to shake off. There are so many versions of this available. So much so that any idea of retirement in the rather traditional sense of giving up work and becoming a pensioner seems old-fashioned and inappropriate, almost an indulgence. Work is where we get our role, our meaning and purpose, and our status. 'What do you do?' is a hugely loaded question. The answer 'I am retired' is often a conversation stopper or prompts the supplementary 'What *did* you do?' This helps the enquirer to place and contextualise us. The better and more philosophical question of 'Who are you?' is rarely asked. Retirement from work prompts this question, however, even if it is unspoken: 'Who am I, how am I going to be in this next stage?'

Changes in social context: varieties and demands of retirement

'Retirement' is an idea serving as a natural staging post in our 'ageing-journey' metaphor. The idea of the retirement pension, introduced by Bismarck, was to give 'old' people, who were worn out from work, a year or so of free time and rest before they died. The assumption (and statistical likelihood at that time) was that men would die soon after their 70th birthday and that the pension would start at this time. (This was reduced to 65 later.) The state would therefore provide some kind of financial support for a brief period before their decline and death. This is how pensions evolved. Things have changed somewhat.

Nowadays, it may be almost anachronistic to conform to the stereotypical trajectory of paid full-time employment until aged 65, with a restful pensioned time thereafter. Gradual feminisation of the workforce since 1945, part-time working, job sharing and portfolio approaches, 'zero-hours' contracts and multiple jobs would probably all be unrecognisable to our forebears. This has required government policy to shift the age of retirement, and to extend future generations' working lives.

However, the language of retirement has not yet caught up. Retirement is still presented as a before and after phenomenon, while lived as a process.

Retirement is a changing concept, and a moveable feast. It is also a process. We wonder if it would be better to think of retirement from work as a re-engagement, a realignment of self with the world, a new orientation? Sometimes it is an abrupt end and new beginning, and sometimes a gradual slide into doing things differently, but always a movement into something else.

The seduction of the 'ageless' story

In the pages of any Sunday-paper magazine, we can read about the beautifully toned, financially secure and successful person who considers herself to be 'ageless'. She is now perhaps in her 60s and declares herself to 'love' being 60. She is a well-known figure in the media, consulted over financial matters and featured as the model to which we should aspire. By all accepted measures, this is so, and people have benefited financially for years from her financial acumen and practices. She is adamant that she doesn't want to retire: she's having too much fun, and she takes care to appear regularly in the media, telling us so. She considers herself ageless but we get the feeling she doesn't mean this in the same way that we discussed in an earlier chapter. Popular agelessness seems to mean forever young, forever in the first half. She seems so sure, and we are confused.

People who have worked in the caring sectors perhaps become wearier, and have less ability to accrue wealth and less time to enjoy it. They have seen humanity at its most vulnerable, hopeful and tragic. One size probably can't fit all. We are, above all else, individuals. The social, cultural and economic contexts in which we live our lives do have a direct bearing on our psychological functioning, as we have already discussed. Anxieties about leaving the European Union, the challenge to the liberal values of the 'elites', the rise in calls for independence and America First point to a change in thinking, and consequently in social relationships. The uncertainties generated by those processes for those who are trying to plan for their old age, or to accommodate the old age of others, will have an effect on individual retirement plans.

Retirement dangers

For the Christian person, retirement is one of the greatest opportunities to rethink and re-engage in faith and spiritual journey, but it is also a danger point, when a rush to fill the apparent space with worthy activities and actions may rather miss the point of the opportunity to change. It is also a danger point in the sense of being subject to the expectations of care from other members of the community, family and relatives because of the apparent 'aimless freedom' now enjoyed by the retired person. These expectations can become a problem.

Caring: virtue or vice?

One of the more recent approaches to retired people and the idea of retirement is that it can and should be a time when individuals, having more time, engage in community volunteering of some kind or other. Instead of 'putting their feet up', the young retired should be out there, doing what needs to be done to help community life, particularly in this age of austerity when there is no spare money to pay for these extra community actions and activities. The flames of this particular approach are also fanned by the wish of the young retired to become actively ageless.

Donald Capps, whose work we discussed in Chapter 2, wrote about the spiritual growth we can acquire during our lives. He assigned to the seventh decade the personal struggle between 'generativity' and 'stagnation', with its accompanying virtue of caring. While there is some discussion about what generativity might mean, we call it here 'doing stuff' or 'contributing'. He suggested that it was at this early stage of entry into what we might call the third age that the virtue of caring could be cultivated and developed. Indeed, we know in contemporary society that many people in their 60s are caring for others. We have already mentioned the reliance on family help for older parents. This situation of 'caring' refers to the role potentially occupied by those who have less pressure at work, more time and more ability to focus on a wider caring role. Increasingly, those people are also becoming relied upon for the care of very elderly parents and young grandchildren, as their own children struggle with the stress and demands of a jointly working household. The retired person can find themselves very quickly swept into new routines, demands and responsibilities as their working life reduces.

This pressure to continue 'contributing' is quite overbearing and certainly pernicious. There is a danger that the retiring person swaps one set of expectational demands for another, without giving themselves a chance to reflect and review the options and their own soul wishes and desires.

Christmas letters from retired family and friends are a wonderful example of the somewhat overwhelming pressure to be 'doing stuff'. The copious photos and text about grandparental activities, holidays, community activities and the general 'we are so busy we don't know how we found time to work' approach may suit some, but may oppress others. The soul needs time to heal and grow. The main currency of retirement, apart from actual money to be able to retire, is the use of time.

The wise elder is *both* the community builder – the person who is able to make things happen, who is able to use his or her previously learned skills in the workplace to good effect in the social community – *and* the person who sets boundaries and secures play time for themselves – the person who is able to love their neighbour *and* themselves.

Church life in retirement: retiring Christians

Churches are no strangers to snapping up the skills and talents of the recently retired, and are less familiar with giving people time, space and opportunities to reflect. Indeed, churches are not good at ageing and understanding the ageing process. They focus intensely on youth, and developing youth policies, often assuming that the retired will feed the youth policies. Churches could be offering opportunities for reflection, space and time for the newly retired, so that their onward spiritual journeys can be carefully discerned.

There is a tendency to assume that the direction will be to make more coffee, hold more jumble sales, raise more money for church roofs. This is not to say that this isn't important work, but surely the major work of a religious organisation is to sustain and support the growth of spiritual life and the soul?

A person who has spent a working life dashing in and out of church life, contributing where they can and feeling constrained in the degree to which they can contribute, is now, in their changed work circumstances, able to give more time to the church. Others already fulfilling the roles are perhaps growing weary, and are very keen to pass on these roles. However, what we find is that a growing number of people who are now able to give church serious thought are beginning to rethink their relationship with church. There are, indeed, a group who continue and increase their involvement, manning coffee stations, fundraising, becoming readers, servers and functionaries, attending more regularly as part of their spiritual development. There are also the group who decide that their own spiritual journey takes them away from the structures of church to a different form of service. Both approaches are valid, and can lead to different types of Christian practice. These sorts of tensions within church communities are more common than often supposed, and there is a growing literature documenting and attempting to explain our growing societal tendencies to leave, or to fail to join, church communities, to explain our disenchantment and to link this to a wider social and political context.

The workplace is far from being the only determinant of our emergent different perspectives as we grow towards retirement, and wonder how we will conduct ourselves. Depending on our own psychological processes, over time we develop different attitudes and stances within our church communities. Church, we note, is historically where we might in the past have lived our spiritual life, but now, it seems, our spirituality is hard to distinguish from our psychological function: after all, modern science and our faithful free press have taught us to see our psychological functioning in every domain of life, from sleeping and feeding, through growing and learning, on to partying and even offending. There are much wider choices and many different paths for our spiritual expression these days. This is both good and alarming. Remaining faithful to loving one's neighbour as oneself is, and will always be, a core challenge.

ANGUS and JOSEPHINE's retirement stories

Angus retired at 56, having found that he was becoming anxious about his work. It was a very different era. He had not intended to retire, but a good deal was offered by his company and he took the chance with both hands. He was thrilled. He could hardly believe that he didn't have to return to work after the Christmas retirement party. He experienced absolutely no conflict about not doing paid work. He was already immersed in a community life, which simply expanded to fill his time. He didn't really give it much thought, just enjoyed the process. This suited his personality and it certainly contributed greatly to the life of the community. His church activities also increased, and he became involved in a variety of church-related committees, fundraising and other activities: 'doing stuff'. His work here enhanced the value of the church to others. This active community life dominated his retirement years. However, he did find a creeping reluctance to lead, and to take responsibility. His anxious feeling returned when this was asked of him.

Josephine did not retire in this way. She started to engage differently with her community and withdrew from some more active roles, while still serving the church in a variety of ways. She was used to living on her small missionary stipend, and had never really connected work with money. She started to run a book group linked to the church, and was able to step up her prayer life. Because of the nature of her working life as a lay nun, missionary and teacher, she was able to continue to use her skills and her learning into her retirement, which became a process of constant readjustment as her health deteriorated and as her financial situation became more precarious.

Angus has known Josephine all his life, has sat near to her at countless services in the village church and has served with her on numerous committees. But her prayer life is unknowable to him. As their ageing trajectories became more and more different and obviously so, Angus began to see Josephine's current situation as a predicament, interpreted her smelliness as some kind of personal moral failure to keep herself clean, and agreed with the widely voiced lay opinion that 'she should be in somewhere by now'. He is relieved to hear it when she is admitted to hospital, feeling this, at some sort of inexpressible level, to be a 'cleaning up' of the community and without reference to the personal freedom he takes for granted. Josephine for her part had always been a bit wary of Angus, sensing his undoubted social charms to be the superficial mannerisms of a well-heeled and privileged former public schoolboy; she remains unclear about the meaning he attaches to his church life, interpreting his adherence as that of a social club member, and is dismissive of any idea that his prayer life would be in any way disciplined or comparable to her own.

Both Angus and Josephine had contributed greatly to the social and church life of the community. Both remained concerned about older people, as they themselves started to outlive their contemporaries.

Moral worth and freedom: retirement guilt

Work insidiously becomes not only what we do, but what we are. Making a clear distinction between 'work self' and 'non-work self' doesn't always help. There is a natural roundness to the life course, and a good retirement should naturally complement the working life it accompanies. What we have learnt at work, both about the work and about ourselves, shapes our retirement.

Cultural norms about the meaning and purpose of work are unconsciously imbibed, and become unquestioningly imprinted on our psyches. In Presbyterian and Calvinist cultures, being seen to work in an approved area of merit has been equated with gain in moral worth. In the West, we have for centuries been trading nations, accumulating wealth through empire and exploitation; latterly, our increasingly liberal democracies have put this wealth to social good through progressive social policy, supporting the poor and less privileged. Churches at times have played central roles in delivering these benefits, including ideas of social justice, even-handedness in the law and systems of social and healthcare providing safety nets, not least for our elders amid the seemingly inevitable decline faced in older age. So far, so good. If we already recognise this as the true stuff of our prior working and professional efforts, though, the concrete need to go on serving our neighbours well (as opposed to simply being seen to compete and succeed) may be less pressing for us than for others in retirement. It may not be the best mode in which to develop and express our creative 'joie de vivre', the joys of creation and of personal freedom which come through so strongly in the gospel references to the day-to-day life of Jesus beyond the 'Wow!' factor of miraculous healings. For some of us, these joys of freedom really are present in the day-to-day run of things.

For others, for whatever reason, there has been, somehow, a need to hold back until retirement, a kind of 'Hang on, I just need to finish this' approach, separating us from healthy playfulness. As the saying goes, life is not a rehearsal, and John Donne's death shroud, present around us from the time in our mothers' wombs, continues to tighten... In other words, we must all seize the day: different things will appeal to different people in retirement according to what (in the way of service) has gone before.

'All work and no play made Jack a dull boy': making changes

We often joke that, on our deathbeds, few of us will say, 'I wish I'd spent more time in the office', usually meaning that we think we should be trying to have a bit more fun. One crucial challenge in our 50s and 60s is that we start to ask ourselves just how satisfying our working lives are, what we should continue to pursue and what we think should be left to us in 'life's afternoon'. For some of us, the real fun and stimulation we had through work has subdued over time, as we realise that we don't change the world so very much; recognising this, we can look firstly and professionally to the small things, then to retirement as an opportunity to do things differently, to change ourselves instead of the world, perhaps simply to change our work arrangements to allow some more flexibility, or at least a different range of challenges. *Now* is always the time to make the changes. While we might need to go on working to generate some necessary income, particularly in an era of shrinking pensions, it needn't be the *same* work; stimulation, our need for novelty and our drive to social contribution all need to be weighed, particularly if work to date has been mundane or boring or has seemingly become disconnected from what we might see as the 'greater good'.

Freedom

We will all have had different lifetime experiences, both within and outside the workplace. These will duly affect our view of life and its possible meanings, impacting on our understandings of our health, our finances and our family situation, and will colour our views on what we can reasonably hope for or expect from the remainder of our lives. We have been led to believe ourselves to be part of a 'big society', and our work, family and wider societal experience might have reinforced this.

Orthodoxy and diversity

'Do the difficult things while they are easy and do the great things while they are small. A journey of a thousand miles must begin with a single step' (Chinese proverb). Changes that start out small can become very large over time: if we think back to our developing embryo from Chapter 2, the changes that form limbs and a spine in the very early days of life are small, but hugely determinant of things to come. So it is with all life: a decision made in early life to marry, or to work at a certain occupation, carves out one path and precludes others. Decisions about family, marriage, disability and retirement mean that we are each on an individual path in relation to ageing and retirement. We remind ourselves of Jung's admonition that 'what was great in the morning [of life] will be little at evening, and what in the morning was true, at evening will have become a lie'.

The making of decisions in life, for which we alone are responsible, may nevertheless be of momentous importance, and sometimes we are resistant to taking those decisions, preferring instead to attribute them to others whom we can subsequently blame. It takes maturity to resist this temptation. It takes strength of character to resist the potentially traumatic impact of the opinions of those around us, even if those orthodoxies might place huge limits on future potential. In resisting the orthodoxies, however, can come the developing strength of character to allow creative divergence from potentially stifling social norms, and the ultimate fulfilment of Christian mission, particularly when the difficult decisions are taken prayerfully.

Retirement allows diversification in respect of Christian or humanitarian service and mission: what we might have yearned to do in early life may now become possible because of new freedom from responsibility, from financial commitments in earlier life, from the simple constraining effect of the nine-to-five. Freedom from these things liberates us, and gives us opportunity for new orientations. We don't have to do things any particular way just because we are Christians. Our reference point is our faithful wrestle with God as we rediscover ourselves, and we hope that our church life can help us with some of that.

Change and renegotiation of self in retirement have repercussions for the way we might care for those older than us. If we accept the idea that the renegotiation is a continuous process as ageing presents change and challenges, then it is important to allow those older people we care for and about to be themselves as well. Imposing rules and restriction in the name of safety is demoralising for all, and shuts down creativity. For instance, seeing activity and entertainment as an essential part of care is in itself an imposition. Josephine's internal activity is sufficiently demanding. She doesn't need to go to basket-weaving groups to give her meaning and pleasure. Others do. Inactivity is a relative concept. Having to fill time with 'doing stuff' in order to feel that care is taking place is oppressive if not given the thought it deserves. Being alert to the dark shadow side of the 'Protestant' ethic, where works are seen as a way of defining value, applies as much to carer as to cared-for. The spiritual care of elders is as much about accompaniment as it is about activity.

Chapter 10

Practising ageing: choosing, believing, trusting

Abraham believed and hoped, even when there was no reason for hoping, and so became 'the father of many nations'... He was then almost one hundred years old; but his faith did not weaken when he thought of his body, which was already practically dead, or of the fact that Sarah could not have children. His faith did not leave him, and he did not doubt God's promise; his faith filled him with power, and he gave praise to God. He was absolutely sure that God would be able to do what he had promised.

ROMANS 4:18–21

I am now giving you the choice between life and death, between God's blessing and God's curse, and I call heaven and earth to witness the choice you make. Choose life. Love the Lord your God, obey him and be faithful to him, and then you and your descendants will live long in the land that he promised to give your ancestors, Abraham, Isaac, and Jacob.

DEUTERONOMY 30:19–20

This final chapter brings together the different strands that have been running through the previous chapters, considers some practical ways in which we (as Christians) can 'do' ageing, and shows how we can shape a positive, hopeful approach. We have reached the end of our discussion, and yet there still seems more to say. In this chapter, we want to take stock, and to think about what our discussion so far implies with regard to our practice.

Adaptive capacity

A few years ago, we directed a small project involving ordained ministers of the Christian church from different denominations.[97] The primary objective was to encourage these ministers to carry out their own piece of research, and thereby to teach them something about qualitative research methods. The focus in each case was on the spiritual care of older people. The research question was: 'Are there particular spiritual needs experienced by older people?' To answer this, the ministers, as researchers, asked a group of older people, drawn from their church congregations, three things at interview: how they were approaching their old age; what coping strategies they had; and what would help them.

The subsequent discussions we had with the ministers about their gathered data, and what they made of these findings, were most illuminating. The degree to which the ageing journey was reported by the respondents as a process of *decline* was noteworthy. The ageing process was summarised by the participants as involving a narrowing and shrinking of horizons and opportunities, loss, a need for intimacy, a wobbly balance between coping and not coping, and changes in role within society and family and individually. None of this was surprising. What *was* surprising was that the ministers, acting as researchers, were *surprised*. The experience of asking the questions had seemingly made them think, anew perhaps, more deeply certainly, about what kind of spiritual care might actually be helpful. Strikingly, the feedback data suggested that there were two types of adaptation required: *resources*, which could be adapted to meet the changing needs (external adaptation); and *adaptive attitude* (internal adaptation), the kind of internal, attitudinal change that we have been suggesting is necessary in this book.

The study found that the important resources for older people included family, nature (being outside, gardens, parks), spousal relationships, community support and involvement in the church. These were the building blocks of comfortable ageing, but the *relationship* between the individual and these resources had to be continually monitored and negotiated. For instance, the adaptation of the family to the ageing person, and vice versa, required sensitive handling and a vision of expectations on both sides. Similarly, with the resource of the church, establishing what it was about the church that helped the older person, and then trying to facilitate that, was an important part of maintaining links with the church.

As regards the attitude of the ageing person, the data suggested that there was a need to have an adaptive attitude to faith, since our understandings of faith change over time. There needed to be a intentional effort to look forward, review memories and find purpose. The study showed that being adaptive, both internally and externally, was a crucial part of ageing well. The spiritual caring tasks were to help the adaptation process, both by manipulating and recruiting external resources, and by encouraging discussion and thought about faith, memories and life meaning. The spiritual task was, therefore, primarily to encourage adaptive attitudes, which of course means in turn that the spiritual caregiver must also cultivate adaptive attitudes herself.

Diagram 1 shows these findings in a different form and points out that good spiritual care must include encouragement of adaptation both internally and externally.

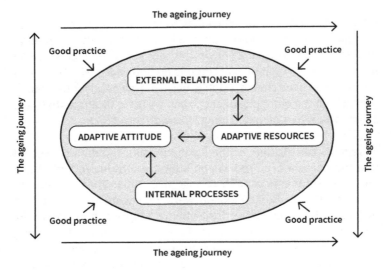

Diagram 1: The ageing journey

Angus and Josephine were both required to be adaptable and were helped in this task by family and friends and professional carers.

ANGUS and JOSEPHINE – continuing their stories

Angus and Josephine's earthly lives have come to an end. Angus died at the age of 90 in his own home, after a relatively short spell of disability, physical diminishment and discomfort. At the time of his death, he was receiving care and support from his wife, children and paid carers, who helped with his daily bodily needs and general activities of daily living. He was still enjoying music and listening to the cricket and the football. He remained able to greet visitors with warmth, and to take some pleasure from his surroundings. We cannot know his actual experience of his death, of course, but his demeanour and attitude seemed calm and resigned, and clearly he was surrounded by people who loved him and who had his best interests at heart. A good death, then? Certainly, a long life well lived.

Angus was mourned and celebrated in equal parts. His death was a relief, as it often is, to his nearest family because his decline had rendered him without much capacity for independence and quality of life. His church funeral service was well attended, and he had previously chosen some rousing hymns for the mourners to sing. He had been a long-standing member of the local church, and the vicar knew him well. Different family members and friends contributed to the service, and there was a delicious tea with chocolate cake and sparkling wine at his home afterwards. As is so often the case at a funeral, people began to tell stories about Angus. A variety of props from previous parties, diaries and photos were unearthed by a variety of family and friends after his death. People were left feeling saddened, but strangely encouraged, by his passing. Good stories were told of him at his funeral and afterwards, and a variety of 'typical Angus events' recalled with much laughter. In the days that followed, Angus' family and friends rallied around the bereaved, and confirmed the value of his life by remembering him with great affection. As time passed, the stories of Angus became incorporated into the story of the village in which he had lived, and into the story of the family he had joined, produced and nurtured. Memories of other family members and other village dwellers were prompted by these stories; whole tracts of new story emerged. Memories of Angus and his life and relationships with others became remembered and renarrated.

These psychological events had the effect of comforting those who felt his absence most keenly, and perhaps placed him more accurately and firmly in their hearts and minds. The 'Angus story retold' became a new tale with additions and adjustments following the process of his death and its marking. Remembering Angus became much more than just remembering Angus *because of these modifications to his context*. The acts of remembrance allowed people's various values, attitudes and approaches to life to be rehearsed, renewed and readopted; Angus lived on in the minds of his friends and family, each of whom of course held a slightly different 'remembered Angus' in their mind. Practices were adjusted in the light of the 'Angus story'. Such processes are universal and continuous, and influence and incorporate both the unborn and the long dead as life's story marches on.

Much the same applied in the demise of Josephine, despite her lack of immediate family. Josephine died in a residential nursing home where she lived against her will, as we know. She had wanted to stay at home, but her situation was too precarious to be tolerated. In her last days, she made a friend of the care attendant who had earlier 'tidied away' (to put it politely) her prayer beads. This young woman had been slowly drawn to Josephine, and had gradually begun to realise the importance of her prayer life. The two had had intimate discussions during times of personal body care, which had stayed with the young care attendant. She had started to take an interest in Josephine's story, and found out through genuine interest enough about Josephine's long life to start to make more sense of her. Josephine's cousin's daughter had also made the effort to visit in the last few weeks of her life, and this had contributed to the storytelling and building of a more complete picture. The cousin had brought old photos and other objects, generating responses and perhaps triggering memories through Josephine's direct sense perceptions. The care attendant reported this to other staff, and a more general awareness of the richness of Josephine's life began to blossom. Josephine slipped away over several days and was generally accompanied during this period either by her cousin's daughter, the young care attendant or her neighbours, who visited regularly. Josephine was alone at the time of her actual death, but it was felt by all concerned that she had enjoyed and valued the accompaniment she had received.

For all her visitors and carers, Josephine had in her last few months finally become a special, unique individual. She had been able to transmit a calm and a conviction that deeply touched and helped others. During these last days, Josephine had indicated her wishes for a very simple funeral and for a 'natural' burial. Arrangements were duly made, and a surprising number of people came to pay their respects to her. The young care attendant wrote something about her, and made up a short prayer. She read these at the funeral. Favourite flowers adorned her simple coffin. A good death and a life well lived? Again, Josephine's life became a story that wove itself into the fabric of others' hearts, into the stories of residents in the home, and into the remembrances of the community. The historical accuracies (or otherwise) of these stories told after death were quite incidental to the way in which they had an impact, enlivening and encouraging others as they did.

Life goes on

So what we seem to find with the account of these two deaths and their aftermath is that both Angus and Josephine in some way *lived on*. In their extreme old age, dying and deaths, they provided those who were to live on beyond them with courage and hope, and above all with examples, methods or models of life, through stories of life. The telling of the stories concerning these two very old people was a spiritual act which had profound consequences for those who told, and for those who listened. It changed the landscape of both the future and the past.

The ability to rewrite stories and to improve them is as ancient a practice as storytelling itself. Rewriting or reconstructing is an important part of learning, by which we can be comfortable with ourselves and thus accept the past, the future and our difficulties while journeying. In our biographical examples, Angus' children could, through story, reconstruct their father, could renegotiate him and their relationship with him in their minds, and could take him with them into their futures and the futures of their own children and grandchildren. Later generations would never meet Angus, but would know of him and about him through story. Their lives would thus be influenced by knowledge of him. We also see that Josephine had a profound effect on her young care attendant, who would go on to write about good practice in residential care and who would, in her turn, learn about how to grow old with grace.

Josephine and Angus' stories are both what we might call 'good stories'. Both provided imaginative guidance, symbolism, continuity and encouragement for those around them; neither story offers real negativity, suggestion of failure or loss of meaning. What if we had considered the death of a young person in violent circumstances, where the adjustments of those left behind were more demanding, even devastating? What if murder or culpability was involved, where a sense of injustice or need for redress prevailed? Although these are hard, even harsh, questions, we believe that the issues remain fundamentally the same, with strength and virtue required to face change, however profound. Sometimes stories are harder to improve, demanding of us even greater compassion, and sometimes, to understand, we must discipline ourselves to attempt to get a grasp on complex medical scientific issues and technologies. Nowhere is this more necessary than when mental disorder has been involved in an illness trajectory, and as the march of neuroscientific progress closes the gaps in our understanding. Death, it seems, may be only the dawning of our understanding.

Summary and conclusion: putting principle into practice

In the previous pages, we have suggested and discussed some key themes about ageing that we hope help us think about what it might mean to be an ageing Christian. We started by acknowledging that ageing is a universal process, experienced uniquely. We have suggested that one of the difficulties of ageing for us all is that we tend to consign it to others, rather than to embrace it ourselves. In accepting our own ageing, we start the journey towards ageing well, and can thus help others to age well. We have, we hope, shown that ageing can be a joyful process of coming to terms with our own selves, and learning to live in humility, using a different set of criteria from today's apparent computer-age 'default factory settings' of productivity, achievement and wealth. If we can diminish power and money as values and replace them with true character virtues, then perhaps we can retrieve what Christians have learnt to call 'gospel values'. This, we think, is what our friend David Ogston meant by 'living without triumph': without expectation of reciprocity, of worldly reward; without a default stance of 'What's in it for me?' We still need to live in the world, and the world demands its pound of flesh; we still need money to survive, and we still need certain wily skills to negotiate our way through humanity's darker side: to avoid and defeat the serpent, perhaps. So our paths are difficult ones.

We have recognised that ageing will involve suffering, but we know that the suffering itself can be converted into something more creative by embracing the idea of actively reinterpreting, and by making changes. Ageing involves change, either willing or reluctant; we can choose to take an active or a passive stance. One of the big choice options in the second half of life is to revalue *being* rather than *doing*, and in so choosing to recreate some of our youthful ambitions to 'stand and stare'. In this process of choice, it is open to us to sharpen up our curiosity about life, and to keep learning about how things are and can be. The way is open to us to retrieve some of our childlike innocence and enjoyment, even in the face of suffering, through letting ourselves relinquish the control that we have earlier demanded or seen as our right, even our duty, to assume. While one dominant pattern in the psychology of ageing is to become more anxious, we are encouraged (through the gospel) to put aside anxiety, and to have faith and trust with Julian of Norwich that 'all shall be well'.

We also know that sometimes other people (and organisations, including families) can get in the way of our ageing well, despite their good intentions. As a 'carer' for older people or as an older person (and sometimes as both), it is important not to get in the way of each other's active engagement with ageing. Rules and regulations, paradigms, assumptions and stereotypes are sometimes very helpful in our making sense of the world, but they can also restrict our view of the 'far-off land' to which we are heading, and can make the journey more perilous. We have suggested that our institutions of social policy, health, economics, religion and family are all both helpful and harmful to our journey, and that they should be carefully navigated to get the best from them. (And even more care is needed over our lifetimes to give of our best into them.) A wariness of institutions is a healthy attitude to cultivate. In so thinking, we are perhaps better able to work on developing our personal virtues as we walk through life. We have looked at the acquisition of these virtues, useful as they are in this earthly life; we confirm from the work of Erikson, Capps and others that there are opportunities to acquire such virtues in every stage of this life; and we are assured by no less an author than C.S. Lewis that, *without* these virtues, no possible external conditions could make us happy with the deep, unshakeable kind of happiness that God intends us to have.

Practising discipleship

While we have talked a little here about spirituality and the serving of others, acknowledging the wide application of these ideas in all faiths and none, there seems to be room to continue in an overtly Christian spiritual vein and to turn briefly but specifically now to Christian discipleship. Former Archbishop Dr Rowan Williams, in his lovely short book *Being Disciples*,[98] talks of the salience of our being 'alive in the Spirit', and focuses his readers' attention on four developmental areas of spirituality relevant to this. One is *growth*, and a lifelong sense of always moving forward, despite the discomforts. A second is that discipleship requires of us some degree of *self-knowledge*. We hope that our own short book has provided at least a stimulus to the introspection required to open up these areas in relation to ageing. Williams also emphasises the need for stillness, long practised historically by Christian disciples but all too readily ignored by many of us in today's pressurised world; we, given our shared interests in serving the elderly, might usefully wonder just how much time we spend in reflection and prayer, and how such time given might ultimately enrich what we are able directly to offer to the people around us, those whom we seek to help.

Williams concludes his invaluable guide by reflecting on the joy available to us in the everyday, but also on how easily this joy is eclipsed by nervousness. We smiled when we read this: Rowan Williams has obviously been to the same hospitals, the same care homes, the same bedsides as us. Anyone with any experience of caring for the elderly, or of working in institutions, will recognise this 'nervousness', perhaps even angrily, and at best with a wry smile. The fact that our tasks may be hard does not mean that they should not be attempted. Williams ends by telling us that these four areas of his, these four endeavours, are what keep us all human and what keep us going. We heartily agree.

There are many ways in which spiritual care for older people can be practised. The Anna Chaplaincy programme sponsored by The Bible Reading Fellowship has a particularly good set of resources, which are available online.[99] The important aspect of all good spiritual care for older people is, however, underpinned by the encouragement to be flexible and adaptive in response to whatever the ageing journey throws up.

Last word

Thank you for reading this book. We hope that you can take on some of its content, and that you will find it useful in your own ageing journey and in the work that you do with others. C.S. Lewis once famously wrote that we read to know that we are not alone: this book is intended to convey our hope for you in your travels and care of others.

Two blessings for old age

We end our book with two blessings for old age. One is ancient and the other a passage from a very contemporary writer, Mimi Spencer.

May the light of your soul mind you.
May all of your worry and anxiousness about becoming old
*   be transfigured.*
May you be given wisdom for the eye of your soul
To see this beautiful time of harvesting.
May you have the commitment to harvest your life
To heal what has hurt you, to allow it to come
Closer to you and become one with you.
May you have great dignity, may you have a sense
*   of how free you are,*
And above all may you be given the wonderful gift
*   of meeting the eternal light, and beauty that is within you.*
May you be blessed, and may you find wonderful love
*   in yourself for yourself.*[100]

There is a joy in ageing, though, which sometimes gets lost in the chorus of grumbles. Stand still, breathe deep and you can hear it in your deep heart's core. I reckon it pays to be adaptable, forgiving and capable of reinvention. It's the half-time whistle, a time to regroup, embrace the changes and own your years, for now you are older and have peace of mind.[101]

Notes

1 From Douglas Abrahams (ed.), *The Book of Joy* (Avery, 2016), pp. 207–208, which reports a meeting between Archbishop Desmond Tutu and His Holiness the Dalai Lama.

2 Erik and Joan Erikson, *The Life Cycle Completed* (extended version) (W.W. Norton and Co., 1998).

3 Helen Small, *The Long Life* (Oxford University Press, 2007), p. 21.

4 David Ogston, *Scots Worship: Advent, Christmas and Epiphany* (St Andrews Press, 2014), pp. 10–14.

5 Richard Rohr with Mike Morrell, *The Divine Dance: The Trinity and your transformation* (SPCK, 2016).

6 Steve Aisthorpe, *The Invisible Church: Learning from the experiences of churchless Christians* (St Andrew Press, 2016).

7 Paul Heelas, Linda Woodhead, et al., *The Spiritual Revolution: Why religion is giving way to spirituality* (Blackwell, 2005).

8 See **www.melanie-klein-trust.org.uk**. This website introduces her work and key concepts and is a good resource for further enquiry.

9 Carl Jung, *Collected Works*, Vol. 8 'Structure and dynamics of the psyche' (Bollingen Series), p. 399, paragraph 784.

10 Comment from James Woodward in April 2017, Church House.

11 Wanda Nash, *Come Let Us Age: An invitation to grow old boldly* (BRF, 2017), p. 16.

12 T.S. Eliot, 'Little Gidding' in *Four Quartets* (Harcourt, 1943).

13 John Bowlby's work as the 'pioneer of attachment theory' can be viewed on DVD as well as read about in numerous articles. We have chosen one of his publications as an example of his work. He was a mid-20th-century British psychologist who influenced a generation of health and social care professionals. He died in 1990. He wrote a three-volume account of his work called *Attachment and Loss* (Hogarth), completing the last volume in 1981 called 'Loss, sadness and depression'.

14 Donald Winnicott was a contemporary of Bowlby and was interested in what he called 'good enough mothering'. His work was also hugely influential. See Donald Winnicott, *Collected Papers: Through paediatrics to psychoanalysis* (Karnac, 1992).

15 Sue Gerhardt, *Why Love Matters: How affection shapes a baby's brain* (Routledge, 2015).

16 Donald Capps, *The Decades of Life: A guide to human development* (Westminster John Knox Press, 2008).

17   From 'Son of God, eternal Savior' (1893) by Somerset Corry Lowry (1855–1932).

18   Sue Gerhardt, *The Selfish Society* (Simon and Schuster, 2010).

19   C.S. Lewis, *Mere Christianity* (William Collins, Signature Classics edition, 2016), p. 81.

20   See **family.jrank.org/pages/1446/Sandwich-Generation-Definition.html**.

21   C.S. Lewis, *The Screwtape Letters* (Geoffrey Bles, 1942), p. 135.

22   Carlo Rovelli, *Seven Brief Lessons on Physics* (Riverhead Books, 2016).

23   Attributed to Cesare Pavese (1908–50).

24   Erik Erikson and Joan Erikson, *The Life Cycle Completed*.

25   Elaine Cumming and William Henry, *Growing Old: The process of disengagement* (Basic Books, 1961).

26   John Wallis Rowe and Robert L. Kahn, *Successful Ageing* (Dell, 1999).

27   Paul Baltes and Margaret Baltes, *Successful Ageing: Perspectives from the behavioral sciences* (Cambridge University Press, 2008).

28   A. Antonovsky, *Health, Stress and Coping* (Jossey-Bass, 1979).

29   Lars Tornstraum, *Gerotranscendence: A developmental theory of positive ageing* (Springer Publishing, 2005).

30   Baltes and Baltes, *Successful Ageing*.

31   Pat Thane, *Old Age in English History: Past experiences, present issues* (Oxford University Press, 2000).

32   J. Gordon Harris, *God and the Elderly: Biblical perspectives on ageing* (Fortress Press, 1987) – part of the Overtures to Biblical Theology series.

33   Viktor E. Frankl, *Man's Search for Meaning* (Ebury Publishing, 2004).

34   Corrie ten Boom, *The Hiding Place* (Hodder and Stoughton, 1971).

35   See **literariness.wordpress.com/2016/03/21/claude-levi-strauss-concept-of-bricolage**.

36   Thomas R. Cole, *The Journey of Life* (Cambridge University Press, 1992), p. xviii.

37   Chaim Potok, *The Chosen* (Simon and Schuster, 1967), p. 217.

38   This paraphrases Scott Peck's opening lines in *The Road Less Travelled* (Arrow Books, 1990).

39   For a brief summary of the issues, refer to H. Mowat and M. O'Neill, *Spirituality and Ageing: Implications for the care and support of older people* (IRISS, 2013). See **www.iriss.org.uk/resources/insights/spirituality-ageing-implications-care-support-older-people**.

40   See **www.itv.com/drama**.

41   W.B. Yeats, *The Collected Poems of W.B. Yeats* (Wordsworth Editions, 1994).

42   Teilhard de Chardin's complex work is rendered manageable and practical in this web page: **www.spiritualpractice.ca/welcome/how-can-my-ageing-become-a-spiritual-practice/a-spirituality-of-diminishment**.

43   Paul Tournier, *Creative Suffering* (SCM Press, 1982).

44   Richard P. Johnson, *The Meaning of Aging*. See **www.senioradultministry.com**.

45   Marcel Proust, quoted in Kathleen Woodward, *Ageing and Its Discontents: Freud and other fictions* (Indiana University Press, 1991), p. 59.

46   Dietrich Bonhoeffer, *The Cost of Discipleship* (SCM Press, 1990), p. 35.

47   Pat Thane (ed.), *The Long History of Old Age* (Thames and Hudson, 2005), p. 299.

48   Woodward, *Ageing and Its Discontents*, p. 59.

49   The Venerable Bede quoted on a plaque at the Metro station at Jarrow, Tyne and Wear. This is a famous extract from Bede's *Ecclesiastical History*. It is a comment made to King Edwin, who is trying to decide whether to become a Christian, by one of his chief advisors.

50   David Oswald and Andrew Blanchflower, 'Is wellbeing U-shaped over the life cycle?', *Social Science and Medicine*, 66.8 (April 2008), pp. 733–49.

51   Yeats, *Collected Poems*.

52   James Hillman, *The Soul's Code: In search of character and calling* (Bantam Books, 1997).

53   Neville Symington, *A Different Path: An emotional autobiography* (Karnac Books, 2016).

54   Gerard W. Hughes, *God in All Things* (Hodder and Stoughton, 2003).

55   Chimamanda Adichie in a TED Talk. See **www.ted.com/talks/chimamanda_adichie_the_danger_of_a_single_story**.

56   James Hillman, *The Force of Character and the Lasting Life* (Random House, 1999).

57   Melvin A. Kimble, Susan H. McFadden et al., *Ageing, Spirituality and Religion: A handbook*, Volume 1 (Fortress Press, 1995).

58   One example is Harold G. Koenig, *Ageing and God: Spiritual pathways to mental health in midlife and later years* (Haworth Pastoral Press, 1994).

59   See, for example, the Special Edition of the *Scottish Journal of Healthcare Chaplaincy* 16 (2013) which carries several articles about the development of the service.

60   See **www.theguardian.com/world/2016/jan/12/church-of-england-attendance-falls-below-million-first-time**.

61   David Hay, *Something There: The biology of the human spirit* (Darton, Longman and Todd, 2006).

62   Paul Heelas and Linda Woodhead, *The Spiritual Revolution: Why religion is giving way to spirituality* (Blackwell Publishing, 2005).

63   Scott Peck, *The Different Drum* (Arrow Books, 1990).

64   Madlove: A designer asylum, see **www.artsadmin.co.uk/events/3926**.

65   See Professor Sir Simon Wessely's blog: **www.simonwessely.com/index.php/blogs** (March 2017).

66   P. Townsend, *Poverty in the United Kingdom* (Allen Lane and Penguin Books, 1979).

67   Centre for Ageing Better, **www.ageing-better.org.uk**.

68   Elinor Newall, Belinda Dewar, et al., 'Cumulative trivia: a holistic conceptualization of the minor problems of ageing', *Primary Health Care Research and Development* 7.4 (October 2006).

69   Tony Robinson and Sally Magnusson as carers. Margaret Thatcher, Terry Pratchett, Ronald Reagan, Prunella Scales all lived with or are living with dementia.

70   John Swinton, *Dementia: Living in the memories of God* (Eerdmans, 2012).

71   Tom Kitwood, *Dementia Reconsidered: The person comes first* (Open University Press, 1997).

72   Richard Rohr, *Falling Upward* (SPCK, 2012).

73   Francis Fukuyama, *Trust: The social virtues and the creation of prosperity* (Simon and Schuster, 1995).

74   Margaret Drabble, *The Dark Flood Rises* (Canongate, 2016), p. 227.

75   Mark Buchanan, *Things Unseen* (Multnomah Publishers, 2002).

76   Small, *The Long Life*, p. 21.

77   James Hollis, *Finding Meaning in the Second Half of Life* (Gotham Books, 2005).

78   Ernest Hemingway, *True at First Light* (Arrow Books, 2004). This quote is taken from an African saying.

79   Iain McGilchrist, *The Master and His Emissary: The divided brain and the making of the Western world* (Yale University Press, 2009).

80   Woodward, *Ageing and its Discontents*, p. 8.

81   C.G. Jung, *Collected Works*, Vol. 8, 'The structure and the dynamics of the psyche' (Routledge, 1960), p. 399, paragraph 784.

82   Hughes, *God in All Things*, pp. ix, x, respectively.

83   David Hay and Rebecca Nye, *The Spirit of the Child* (Jessica Kingsley Publishers, 1998).

84   William Wordsworth, 'Intimations of Immortality'.
See **www.bartleby.com/101/536.html**.

85   Sarah Hills, *Reconciliation and Restitution through the Eucharist* (Doctoral thesis, Durham University, 2015).

86   John Dempster, 'On Humility', *Highland Weekly News*, 23 November 2015.

87   See **www.mediapost.com/publications/article/231356/the-beginnings-of-ageless-marketing-ii.html**.

88   Aisthorpe, *The Invisible Church*.

89   Ben Okri, *The Commission on the Future of Multicultural Britain*, 2000. Retrieved 7 May 2017 from AZQuotes.com: **www.azquotes.com/quote/789417**.

90   Joan Chittister, *The Gift of Years: Growing older gracefully* (Darton, Longman and Todd, 2008).

91   Elizabeth MacKinlay, *The Spiritual Dimension of Ageing* (Jessica Kingsley Publishers, 2001).

92   Koenig, *Ageing and God*, pp. 284–94.

93   Jonathan Sacks, *Not in God's Name: Confronting religious violence* (Hodder and Stoughton, 2015).

94   Jung, *Collected Works* Vol. 8, p. 399, paragraph 784.

95   Borrowed and adapted from Wikipedia: **en.wikipedia.org/wiki/Protestant_work_ethic**.

96   Walter Brueggemann, *Spirituality of the Psalms* (Augsburg Fortress, 2002).

97   Suzanne Bunniss et al., 'The Spiritual Care of Older People', *SACH Journal* 13.1 (2010).

98   Rowan Williams, *Being Disciples: Essentials of the Christian life* (SPCK, 2016).

99   See **www.thegiftofyears.org.uk/what-anna-chaplain**.

100 John O'Donohue, *Anam Cara: Spiritual wisdom from the Celtic world* (Bantam Books, 1997), p. 242.

101 Mimi Spencer, 'I'm middle-aged: surely some mistake?' *The Times, Magazine Supplement* (29 April 2017).

This book approaches dementia from a number of angles: biological, psychological, sociological, and theological. After an introduction explaining the multifaceted nature of this set of conditions, some possible theological responses are offered to such questions as: what is the nature of human identity? How can someone with severely impaired cognition have a full spiritual life? The book's final two sections are predominantly practical, addressing the spiritual care of the affected individual and how to help churches support affected individuals and their carers.

Thinking of You
A resource for the spiritual care of people with dementia
Joanna Collicutt
978 0 85746 491 0 £9.99

brfonline.org.uk

In this unique book, Wanda Nash, a well-established writer on spirituality in her late 70s, reflects on growing old with faith and a positive spirit. This compelling invitation to grow old boldly – full of her own experiences and insights – includes Wanda's reflection on her encounter later in life with terminal cancer, and her thoughts on coping with the daily challenges of living a Christian life in her illness and in ageing. Demonstrating a profound sense of the value and purposefulness of 'old age', the author's indomitable spirit is matched only by her fresh vision of the love of God in Jesus Christ.

Come, Let Us Age!
An invitation to grow old boldly
Wanda Nash
978 0 85746 558 0 £6.99

brfonline.org.uk

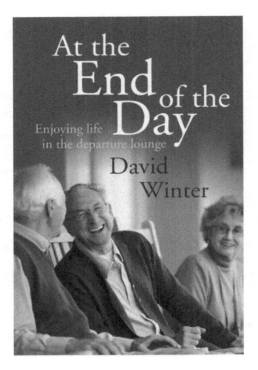

An octogenarian takes a wryly humorous look at what it's like to be old in an era of the relentlessly new. Turning to the Bible, he explores its store of timeless wisdom, encouragement and reassurance about what it has always meant to grow old and be old. The book is structured around a series of fascinating biblical pictures, from the legendary Methuselah to the feisty Sarah and the great leader Moses, from the picture of inevitable decline as the Preacher saw it in Ecclesiastes to the glorious Nunc Dimittis of old Simeon in the temple.

At the End of the Day
Enjoying life in the departure lounge
David Winter
978 0 85746 057 8 £6.99

brfonline.org.uk

The Bible – especially the New Testament – has plenty to say about resurrection and heaven, but many Christians struggle to make sense of what it actually means in practice. David Winter's accessible book explores the biblical teaching on what happens after death and considers what difference this can make to our lives here and now. He also shows how we can present what we believe about eternity as a source of hope to our sceptical, anxious world.

Heaven's Morning
Rethinking the destination
David Winter
978 0 85746 476 7 £7.99

brfonline.org.uk

The Gift
of Years

Resourcing the spiritual journey
of older people

BRF's The Gift of Years programme aims to equip churches to support older people wherever they may be – in residential care, congregations, in their own homes and in the community. At the heart of The Gift of Years is a growing network of Anna Chaplains.

Find out more at **thegiftofyears.org.uk**

 brf.org.uk